THE SMART, SAVVY YOUNG CONSUMER
HOW TO SAVE AND SPEND WISELY

Pat Foran

KNOWLEDGE BUREAU
NEWSBOOKS

WINNIPEG, MANITOBA, CANADA

Pat Foran

THE SMART, SAVVY YOUNG CONSUMER
How to Save and Spend Wisely

Printed and bound in Canada

Library and Archives Canada Cataloguing in Publication

Foran, Pat
    The smart savvy young consumer : how to save and spend wisely / Pat Foran.

ISBN 978-1-897526-75-0

1. Teenagers—Finance, Personal. 2. Young adults—
Finance, Personal. 3. Finance, Personal. I. Title.

HG179.F674 2011   332.024   C2011-906618-1

Published by:
Knowledge Bureau, Inc.
187 St. Mary's Road, Winnipeg, Manitoba Canada R2H 1J2
204-953-4769 Email: reception@knowledgebureau.com

Publisher: Evelyn Jacks
Editor: Nicole Chartrand
Cover and Page Design: Sharon Jones

Dedication

This book is dedicated to my beautiful daughters
Lisa, Vanessa and Sarah. May you have wonderful, joyous lives
filled with happiness and remain free from the stress of financial problems.
Watch your spending and keep saving girls!

Love, Dad

ACKNOWLEDGEMENTS

I would like to thank all the people I have met and interviewed over the years who have shared their stories about financial issues. I want to thank our Federal Finance Minister Jim Flaherty for choosing me to be on the Financial Task Force for Financial Literacy which was an amazing experience. Thanks as well to Task Force member Evelyn Jacks who encouraged me to write this book. I want to thank my 16 year old daughter Vanessa who took a keen interest in this project and helped in the research and proofreading of this book. I also want to thank the CTV Television Network, my employer of 25 years (where did the time go!) as working for *CTV News* is a job I truly enjoy that allows me to help the people of Canada. I also want to thank my wife Carole for her unending support over the years and my mother Helen Foran who had to be a frugal consumer raising a large family with little to go around. Thanks to you as well for reading this book. I hope it will help you achieve your financial dreams. I wish you all the best in the future!

TABLE OF CONTENTS

Acknowledgements   5

Part One

  1. Why it's Important to Save and Spend Wisely   9
  2. Wisdom from Successful Canadians Young and Old!   13
  3. Financial Literacy—Why it's More Important Than Ever   23
  4. Why Financial Literacy Should be Taught in School   25
  5. Money Advice from Young Canadians   29
  6. So Who are the Canadian Millionaires?   33
  7. So You Want to be a Millionaire—What Does it Take? 35
  8. Are You a Spender or a Saver?   37
  9. Knowing What You're Worth   41
10. Watching Where Your Money Goes   45
11. You Are Your Own Small Business   49
12. Be Cool—Stay in School   53

Part Two

13. Reducing Debt   55
14. Bad Spending Habits   57
15. Good Debt vs. Bad Debt, Understanding Leverage   59
16. Debt Consolidation—Why it Doesn't Always Work   61
17. Money for a Rainy Day—The Emergency Fund   63
18. Paying Off Student Loans   67
19. Trying to Get a Scholarship   71

Part Three

20. Drowning in Debt—Using Credit Responsibly   75
21. Choosing the Right Credit Card   79
22. Lines of Credit—It's Not Your Money!   81
23. Minimum Monthly Payments—Beware   83
24. Your Credit Score—The Most Important Number   85
25. Protecting Your Identity   89
26. Payday Loan Services—A Bad Idea   93
27. Declaring Bankruptcy—Don't Do It   95

Part Four

28. Saving Money—Investing for the Future   99
29. Paying Yourself First   103
30. The Power of Compound Interest   105
31. The Power of Dollar Cost Averaging   109
32. Stocks, Mutual Funds and Exchange Traded Funds   111
33. The Tax Free Savings Account   115
34. RRSPs   119
35. Doing Your Taxes—Advice from an Expert   123
36. Financial Advisors—Do You Need One?   127
37. Life Insurance and Wills—Do You Need Them?   131
38. Be a Smart Shopper—Not an Early Adopter   135
39. Buying Used—Saving Money   137
40. Getting the Best Deal on Your Cell Phone   139
41. TV, Internet and Utilities—Keeping Costs Under Control   143
42. Eating Smart—Trimming the Grocery Bill   145

Part Five

43. Buying a Car—Looking at the Big Picture   149
44. Buying a New Car   153
45. Leasing a Vehicle—Beware   157
46. Buying a Nearly New Car   161
47. Buying a Used Car—Avoiding a Lemon   163
48. Getting the Best Deal on Car Insurance   167

Part Six

49. Buying a Home   171
50. The Rent Trap   175
51. Managing Your Mortgage   177
52. Breaking Your Mortgage   181
53. Home and Tenant Insurance   183
54. Home Renovations—Beware   187

Part Seven

55. Your Future—Being Careful on Facebook and Twitter   189
56. Writing the Perfect Resume   193
57. Asking for a Raise   199
58. Flex Your Social Power   201
59. Giving to Charity—Volunteer Tourism   205
60. Enjoying Your Life!   209

Glossary of Financial Terms   211

Index   216

PART ONE

[1]
WHY IT'S IMPORTANT
TO SAVE
AND SPEND WISELY

It has always been important to be wise with your saving and spending, but for young people today it is now more crucial than ever. Savings rates are at all-time lows, while debt levels are at all-time highs. Many young people feel depressed about their financial situation. They may be saddled with credit card debt, student loans, and are struggling from month to month just to pay the rent. The generation ahead of them doesn't feel much better. Many people in their 30s and 40s are stuck in a rut living from one paycheque to the next. Many seniors are now also taking debt into retirement, retiring with a mortgage, line of credit and credit card debt. For young people today there are also special challenges ahead because their parents or grandparents enjoyed some financial benefits that they may not. Homes purchased when they were in their 20s for $20,000 jumped in value over 30 years to as much as $400,000 or more. The same is true of cottages and even farm land that was $500 an acre 30 years ago, is now selling for $10,000 an acre! Those were the days. Jobs were plentiful, careers were stable and most positions came with a full pension. Stay at a job, work hard and your retirement will be looked after. Well unfortunately for today's youth—times have changed.

But, there is hope. If you start out on the right path, make the right decisions and keep your spending under control you can enjoy a financially secure life which will allow you to live with a lot less stress. It may be hard to believe now but you are actually starting off in a very enviable position. You are beginning with a clean slate, balanced books, and if you make all the right moves when it comes to saving and spending, you can't lose. It's not always easy and temptation lurks around every corner trying to get you to part with your money, but by spending less than you make, being wise with your purchases and not living beyond your means, you can't help but get ahead. It is true that most young people (including myself when I finished school) are not too concerned about saving for the future, mainly because it seems so far away. No one in their 20s wants to picture themselves in their 70s with graying hair, wrinkles and spending time in the garden. For many, the thought of saving for your retirement when you are just moving out of your parent's house, finishing school, buying a car and beginning your first job seems almost ridiculous. However, by developing good habits early you won't have to worry about the future, because if you spend and save wisely throughout your life, your retirement will look after itself.

This is my fourth financial book and the first directed toward younger Canadians. I have worked at *CTV News* for 25 years, 12 of them as a Consumer Reporter. I hear from consumers every day. They call, email and write to me about problems with credit cards, car loans, mortgages, investments, lines of credit, scams, job loss, insurance, identity theft. You name it, I've heard about it. That's why I hope the information in this book will help you become *A Smart, Savvy, Young Consumer*. It is possible to save money, invest wisely, avoid interest costs, maintain a good credit rating, get a good deal on a car, save for a home, pay off your mortgage faster, not overpay for insurance, and most importantly become someone who makes wise decisions about money every day. It can be done and it's not as hard as you might think.

In my last book my favourite catch phrase was "Stop trying to keep up with the Joneses—they're broke!" That remains true today. We are in a consumer driven society where we want things right away, whether it is a big screen TV, the latest tablet computer, luxury cars or designer clothing. We think nothing of laying down a credit card to pay for dining out, expensive vacations or the latest cool shoes. Often we buy things we don't need, to impress people we don't know. As you get older you'll also discover many people look like they have a lot of money, but in fact don't. They may drive luxury cars, live in big houses and take expensive vacations but they could be mortgaged to the hilt, have massive credit card bills and be just two paycheques away from having their financial house of cards collapse.

One of the most important things to remember is—it's not how much money you make, it's how much you save. Singer Michael Jackson amassed a fortune in his lifetime, but died reportedly $400 million dollars in debt. The singer would go on spending sprees and even spent as much as $35 million improving his Neverland Ranch, which featured two railway lines, two helicopter pads, a fire department, a zoo and an amusement park. Millionaires actor Burt Reynolds, singer MC Hammer, actress Judy Garland, actress Kim Basinger, singer Willie Nelson and comedian Sinbad are many high profile people who went broke or declared bankruptcy for various reasons. How could that be when they were worth millions of dollars? Once again, it's because it's not how much you make, it is how you spend and save it. Many people are also under the impression that only poor people have money problems, but there are surgeons making $350,000 a year who can't balance their books. They may be brilliant in the operating room, but not at the bank.

Being wise with your money is not that hard but it does take self-control, discipline and some sacrifice to become and remain debt free. If you are lucky you have had parents who have offered you financial advice through the years. In this book, along with advice from me, you will hear from famous Canadians and experts in the areas of finance, credit, insurance, buying cars and investing for the future. If you want to be financially secure, so you can do what you want in life without having to worry about money, then this book is for you. Money management can appear complicated, but when you know the basics you will find it is not. You too can be *A Smart, Savvy, Young Consumer*, and by being more knowledgeable, you will avoid many of the problems many Canadians are now facing. Let's get started.

[2]
WISDOM FROM SUCCESSFUL CANADIANS YOUNG AND OLD!

I have always been interested in quotations as I feel, in just a few short words, they can sum up what a person has to say about love, money, fame, fortune or whatever the topic may be. In my past books I asked famous and successful Canadians their views on financial advice and what words of wisdom they would pass on to their fellow citizens. Over the years I have come to know the Finance Minister of Canada Jim Flaherty as I live in his riding of Whitby-Oshawa. I often see him at Canada Day festivities where I help out with swearing in ceremonies of new Canadian citizens, something I enjoy doing. It is always great to see the joy on the faces of people as they realize they are now officially Canadian.

Flaherty was at the helm of Canada's financial system during the stock market meltdown in 2008 and had to manage the market fallout and economic uncertainty after. He has not just been recognized for his efforts in Canada, but is respected around the world. In 2009, he was named the *Finance Minister of the Year* by *Euromoney*, a 40-year-old publication devoted to international financial markets. On receiving the award he had this to say:

"While it's an honour to receive this award, it's really a testament to the perseverance of Canadians themselves throughout this global economic and financial crisis. It recognizes how Canadians built a sound economy and worked together to weather the global storm better than most other countries."

Flaherty is not just a powerhouse on the international stage. He and his wife Christine Elliott, who represents Whitby-Oshawa in the Ontario Legislature, are also parents to their 20 year old triplets Quinn, Galen and John. I asked him when he

13

does not have to manage Canada's financial system, what advice he has for his three sons and he had this to say:

> *"My advice to our own sons is first of all, get a good education. Secondly, spend less than you earn so you will have savings and understand the benefits of compound interest. Thirdly, buy a principal residence and pay off the mortgage as quickly as you can and benefit from the tax free capital gain. Finally, be frugal and careful with credit, especially high interest credit cards."*
>
> Jim Flaherty
> The Finance Minister of Canada

Like many Canadians, 20 years ago I read *The Wealthy Barber*, a personal financial book by David Chilton that went on to sell more than two million copies in Canada. In the fictional story, Chilton weaves a small town tale about Roy the barber who has a meagre income, but is still able to amass a fortune by spending less than he earns, investing 10% of his income and living within his means. It took Chilton more than 20 years to write a follow-up, *The Wealthy Barber Returns*. I asked him the best advice he could pass on to young Canadians and he had this to say:

> *"The most valuable financial lesson I've ever learned came not from Warren Buffett or George Soros or John Templeton or any of the other great money minds of our time. Instead it came from regular folk— people who have lived within their means and reached their financial objectives. What is that lesson? Pay yourself first, of course. Yes it's trite, old-fashioned and oft-heard, but it works. We all must save and the best way to do it is through pre-authorized chequing and payroll deductions. Budgeting sounds great in theory but doesn't often work in practice. Basic but key advice—take it off the top (sounds like a barber speaking!)."*
>
> David Chilton
> Author, *The Wealthy Barber Returns*

Canadians actually have a reputation of being careful with money. Even one of Canada's current international teen superstars Justin Bieber, from Stratford, Ontario, who is worth tens of millions of dollars, says he is frugal with money. The 17 year old who was discovered on *YouTube* in 2008 and went on to captivate the world with his singing and dance moves, was raised by his single mother in low income housing. Still, he managed to teach himself to play the piano, drums, guitar and trumpet. When asked about money the teen sensation had this to say:

"I grew up below the poverty line; I didn't have as much as other people did. I think it made me stronger as a person, it built my character. I've got my eye on a few things to spend my money on. I've got my own bank card, but I am really good with money. I don't spend too much at all."

Justin Bieber
Pop Superstar

Comedian Jim Carrey was born in Newmarket, Ontario and went on to become one of the highest paid comedians of all time. He has achieved international success, received two Golden Globes and has earned an estimated 200 million dollars in his career, including 20 million dollars to do *The Cable Guy* which at the time was the largest up-front sum ever paid to a comic actor. You would think the man from *The Grinch Who Stole Christmas*, *Dumb and Dumber* and *Ace Ventura: Pet Detective* might be a big spender, but Carrey had this to say about money:

"I haven't been as wild with my money as somebody like me might have been. I've been very safe, very conservative with investments. I don't blow money. I don't have a ton of houses. I know things can go away. I've already had that experience."

Jim Carrey
Canadian Comedian and Actor

Celine Dion is not just one of Canada's most famous singers; she is arguably the most famous singer in the world with one of the most powerful voices in music today. The youngest of 14 children born in Charlemagne, Quebec, she grew up singing with her brothers and sisters in her parent's small piano bar. Dion is the best-selling Canadian artist of all time and has sold over 200 million albums worldwide. She has amassed a fortune and made *Forbes* list as the fifth richest woman in entertainment worth an estimated 250 million dollars. She recently spent 20 million dollars on a mansion in Florida complete with an aquatic water park. She is known to be extremely generous and had this to say when asked about her spending habits:

"I often buy myself presents. Sometimes I will spend $100,000 in one day in a posh boutique."

Celine Dion
Canadian Singer

Not all Canadians can achieve the status of Justin Bieber, Jim Carrey or Celine Dion, but some are trying. Luke Bilyk is a Canadian actor, born in Scarborough,

Ontario in 1994 who is best known for his role in *Degrassi: The Next Generation* as Drew Torres. He was also in *My Baby Sitter's a Vampire* and has appeared in many episodes of the hit TV show, *The Latest Buzz* as well as *Little Mosque on the Prairie*. I asked the young actor his views on money and advice he would give other young Canadians:

> *"The best piece of advice I have ever received about money was given by my father. His advice was that you should always 'give some, save some and spend some.' I have also learned that it is good to give some away to people in need, food shelters or charities. You should always help the unfortunate with the money that you make, because eventually you will be blessed back or you may need someone to help you out sometime. I have also learned that it is better to purchase some silver or gold than to leave all your paper money in the bank as silver or gold is an investment which never loses its value. Being wise with our money is having an understanding of how it should be used."*
>
> Luke Bilyk
> Actor, *Degrassi: The Next Generation*

I got a chance to meet Craig Kielburger this year and like everyone who has met him, I was very impressed. The 28 year old activist was born in Thornhill, Ontario. In 1995, when he was 12 years old, Kielburger saw a headline in the newspaper that read "Battled child labour, boy, 12, murdered." The story was about a young Pakistani boy who was forced to be a labourer in a carpet factory and was fighting for children's rights when he was killed. Angered by the story, Kielburger began researching child labour and formed a group that would eventually evolve into *Free The Children*, an international organization that now involves more than 45 countries. I asked Kielburger about his own experiences with money when he was growing up.

> *"The best financial lessons I learned were from my mother. In her case, she never said "no" when I wanted a pair of designer jeans, or the newest video game, or any other new item I just "had" to have. Instead, my parents had me earn money to make the purchases by doing good works. I would volunteer at a homeless shelter or a soup kitchen, learning about the far more profound needs of others. When I was finished, my parents handed over the money. They also let me decide what to do with it. In the end, more often than not, I donated the money."*
>
> Craig Kielburger
> Co-Founder, *Free The Children*

16

Now I know Billy Idol is not Canadian. The English rocker was born in Middlesex, England but I've always found him to be an interesting character and I will always remember that the first time I ever came to Toronto was to see a Billy Idol concert. It was quite an adventure for four teenagers from the small town of Lucan, Ontario to pile into my friend Bob's Z-28 Camaro to come to the bright lights of the big city to see a rock concert. Idol (real name William Michael Albert Broad) has had ups and downs in life and has seen his money come and go with the ebb and flow of his career. I got a chance to see him when he was on CTV's *Canada AM* once and I thought his quote on finances was an interesting one.

"It doesn't matter about money; having it, not having it. Or having clothes, or not having them. You're still left alone with yourself in the end."

Billy Idol
Rock Musician

As I mentioned at the beginning of the book I was part of the Federal Government's Task Force on Financial Literacy and I asked my fellow members if they would provide either insights about our travels across Canada with the Task Force or advice for young Canadians. Laurie Campbell is the Executive Director of Credit Canada and the Credit Counselling Service of Toronto and has worked to help people with credit issues for more than 20 years. Campbell says if young people make the right choices early on they can begin their lives on firm financial footing.

"When you're starting off in life, it's like a clean slate, an empty page and you have the opportunity to start out right. It's not complicated, the biggest message I would say is don't think managing money is complicated because it's not."

Laurie Campbell
Executive Director, Credit Canada

Task Force Member Greg Pollock is the President and CEO of Advocis, The Financial Advisors Association of Canada. Pollock also served as the General Secretary of the Ontario English Catholic Teachers' Association from 2001-2008. His advice for young Canadians is short and to the point:

"While money cannot provide happiness, it can go a long way towards lowering stress."

Greg Pollock
President and CEO, Advocis

Task Force Member Janice MacKinnon is a Professor of Fiscal Policy at the University of Saskatchewan. From 1991 to 2001, she was a Cabinet Minister in the Saskatchewan Government and served as Finance Minister during the province's deficit/debt crisis, when Saskatchewan became the first government in Canada to balance its budget in the 1990s. MacKinnon had this observation following our cross country hearings:

"Two surprises for me on the Task Force were discovering how many educated, successful people make bad financial choices and being heartened to hear from so many groups committed to enhancing the financial literacy of Canadians."

Janice MacKinnon
Professor of Fiscal Policy, University of Saskatchewan

Task Force Member Evelyn Jacks is the founder and president of the Knowledge Bureau, a leading national educational institute focused on providing professional development for practicing tax and financial advisors. (The Knowledge Bureau is also the publisher of this book.) Jacks is well known to Canadians as the best-selling author of 45 books on the subject of personal tax and financial planning. She has received numerous awards in recognition of her contributions to excellence in financial education including the prestigious National Canadian Woman Entrepreneur of the Year. I asked what advice she would pass on to young Canadians about managing their money.

"Some of the best financial advice I ever received came from my Mom and Dad, who taught us the difference between wants and needs, how to save money and how to manage debt. It's important to be the boss of your own money, they counselled, with professional assistance, as required. It concerns me that many families are not talking to children about the principles of money management today. In these volatile financial times, financial literacy is a critical life skill, which everyone needs. If Mom and Dad are not talking about it, smart, savvy young consumers need to be proactive and ask more questions, to acquire the knowledge and skills they need to make responsible decisions, with confidence."

Evelyn Jacks
President, The Knowledge Bureau

Task Force Member Bill Schwartz is with Polestar Communications Inc., a firm of educational specialists which developed a financial literacy program for students in British Columbia called *The City*. Schwartz is also involved in examining high school programs across the country to see what students are being taught when it comes to financial literacy. His view is, there is still plenty of work to do.

> *"When we first started writing about financial literacy for high school we found most of the students saw themselves making lots of money and living very well. Their expectations differed significantly from the actual income levels of various occupations in Canada. For most students, their expectations were beyond their reach. That told us that we had to give them solid information about finances to fill the gap in their knowledge and experience and help them acquire good financial management skills so they had a better chance of reaching the lifestyles they aspired to."*
>
> Bill Schwartz
> Principal Polestar Communications Inc.

Task Force Member Ted Gordon is a Financial Security Advisor with Freedom 55 Financial in Ottawa as well as a Professor in the School of Part-Time Studies at Algonquin College where he teaches a non-credit, personal interest course called *Personal Financial Literacy*. Gordon says what young people need to learn early is that they must be in control of their own financial destiny.

> *"I think the best advice that I could pass on to younger people about money would be that they must be in control of their own finances. If you're not, it means someone else is, and that may not ensure the best financial result for you. You can still get expert advice from a financial advisor or mortgage expert, but you are ultimately responsible and bear the financial consequences of those decisions."*
>
> Ted Gordon
> Financial Security Advisor, Freedom 55 Financial

Before I introduce the Chairman of the Task Force on Financial Literacy, I want to give some background which might help provide some insight into his quote. All of us on the Task Force were asked to read the book *Nudge* by authors Richard Thaler and Cass Sunstein. The premise of the book is that we as humans don't always do the right thing even though we know we should. So if banks, insurance companies, governments and businesses could find ways to "nudge" us in the right direction we would make better decisions, sometimes without even realizing it. There is one example that proves this point perfectly, and it is certainly a bit out of the ordinary to say the least.

A men's washroom at the Schiphol Airport in Amsterdam had an issue with cleanliness—as men are not always the best at aiming. It seems men don't always hit the urinal perfectly, because of lack of concentration while going to the bathroom. However, when researchers decided to etch the image of a black housefly into the centre of each urinal, men would see the fly as a target, focus and take aim. Staff for the restroom decided to conduct "fly in urinal trials" and found the fake houseflies reduced spillage by 80%! So, without even knowing it, men were being "nudged" to help make the bathroom cleaner.

The Chairman of the Task Force on Financial Literacy is Donald Stewart, Chief Executive Officer of Sun Life Financial Inc.. Stewart did an excellent job as leader of the Task Force and under his direction we were able to make 30 recommendations, many of which we hope one day can be implemented. Stewart led our meetings with a stopwatch at his side and always kept us focused on the task at hand. I hope Don doesn't mind that I used the urinal example to help explain his quote for a younger audience! Here is what Stewart had to say:

> *"When reflecting on the work of the Task Force, a universal insight that emerged was the fundamental importance of human behaviour. Economists have analyzed the interaction between people and their money extensively in recent years and the overall conclusion is that individual financial decisions are influenced both positively and negatively by how financial choices are presented. Economists call it 'choice architecture'. Research shows that people often need a 'nudge' to make their best choice, such as automatic enrolment in a savings plan. It's these behaviour patterns that need to be part of a financial program design."*
>
> Donald Stewart
> Chief Executive Officer, Sun Life Financial Inc.

As a member of the Task Force on Financial Literacy, I attended the Financial Literacy Summit in Chicago in 2011 and met with members of President Barack Obama's Advisory Council on Financial Capability. It's not just Canadians doing their best to find ways to help make citizens more financial literate. The U.S., mired deep in its own financial troubles, is hoping that if Americans can become more financial literate they can help themselves and in turn help the American economy. Ted Beck is serving with President Obama's Advisory Council and is the President and CEO of The National Endowment for Financial Education. He offered this observation to help young people avoid expensive impulse buys.

"I was told before making any major purchase a wise decision is to sleep on it at least one night. I have always found this to be very useful advice."

> Ted Beck
> Council Member, President Obama's Advisory
> Council on Financial Capability
> The National Endowment for Financial Education

I also got the chance to meet John W. Rogers, Jr. who serves as Chairman of President Obama's Advisory Council on Financial Capability. Rogers is the founder of Ariel Investments, a Chicago based money management firm. He has received numerous awards and recognitions for giving back to the community and trying to help educate young people about financial literacy. Here is his advice for young people:

"My passion for investing started when I was 12 years old when my father bought me stocks for every birthday and every Christmas instead of toys. I believe young people need to learn about investing as early as possible. If you are going to make mistakes, and many of us do, it's best to make them early. Children also need to learn the importance of a job and a savings account."

> John W. Rogers Jr.
> Chair, President Obama's Advisory Council
> on Financial Capability
> Chairman and CEO, Ariel Investments

I thank everyone for these quotes and hope they will be an inspiration as we begin to look at ways to save money, make good financial decisions and invest for the future.

[3]
FINANCIAL LITERACY—
WHY IT'S MORE IMPORTANT
THAN EVER

As the Consumer Reporter at CTV, I receive calls, emails and letters from people every day who have made terrible financial mistakes. They sign contracts without knowing what they are agreeing to, they put down payments on cars they can't afford, and dig themselves into debt they don't know how to get out of. They buy things they don't need, they have bills they can't pay and they often are looking to blame anyone but themselves. However, the truth is that many of the financial mistakes we make are our own fault. That is why financial literacy is more important than ever. Debt levels in Canada are at record levels and while many of us are great at spending money, we are not as great at saving it. It was in 2009 that the federal government commissioned a Federal Task Force to research the state of the Canadian consumer's financial affairs. The Task Force met over two years and in 2010, public hearings for 12 weeks were held across the country in every province and territory. Our job was to research ways to help Canadians become better savers and spenders. I was asked to participate as a task force member because of my role as the Consumer Reporter at *CTV News*. It was a volunteer position for which I was paid one dollar (and I can't spend it because it is encased in glass).

As we crossed the country and met with Canadians, many of the same issues came up—overspending, growing debt loads and lack of basic financial knowledge. Many people were making bad decisions and it didn't seem to matter if they were in British Columbia or Newfoundland. We studied what they were doing in other countries to advance financial literacy and we met with financial groups, student councils, credit counselling officials, charitable agencies, and government officials to see what could be done to make Canadians more financially literate. For the national public hearings I travelled to Yellowknife, Edmonton, Calgary, Saskatoon, Ottawa and Toronto. We did hear that there are Canadians carefully watching the amount of interest they pay, saving for their retirement and paying off their credit card bills every month, but there are others who could be doing so much more to help their financial situation.

So what does this mean for a young person? Well if you can learn proper money management techniques, how to live within your means, avoid overspending and save for the future, you will be so much further ahead than many Canadians are now. Don't think that making a huge salary is the answer either, because we heard that even professionals with six-figure incomes are running into problems despite earning good money. Whether it's a single parent trying to make ends meet, a student facing huge school loans or a person ready to go into retirement, the more money you can keep for yourself, the better off you will be. We, as a Task Force, made 30 recommendations that we feel will help Canadians become more financially literate. Here are the top five recommendations:

1. Appoint a national financial literacy leader
2. Establish a financial literacy advisory council
3. Create a website for independent financial information
4. Integrate financial literacy into all school systems
5. Require clear communication in financial documents

For the complete list of 30 recommendations, other information on the task force and our full report, you can check www.financialliteracyincanada.com.

The Task Force defined financial literacy as having the knowledge, skills and confidence to make responsible financial decisions. Not a day goes by that Canadians do not have to make some kind of financial decision. Some decisions are routine, such as what groceries to buy or whether to pay by cash or by credit card. However, others require more thought, such as deciding where to invest money, where to go to college or university or where and how to take out a first mortgage. As a young person, if you can create good habits for yourself and put some of the wealth building tools in this book to good use, you will be so much further ahead than many Canadians are today. The secret is to start early and as a young person you have time on your side. Like most things in life, learning the hard way is one way to do it. Some people figure out how to manage their money in their 20s, some their 30s, others their 40s or 50s, but the truth is, some don't get it figured out until it's too late. If you can become a *Smart, Savvy Young Consumer*, you will be on the right track to financial success. You will be happier, less stressed and feel better about your finances and, in turn, feel better about your life in general.

[4]
WHY FINANCIAL LITERACY SHOULD BE TAUGHT IN SCHOOL

I believe financial literacy should be taught in school as a stand-alone mandatory course to be completed before a student can graduate from high school. I've been saying it for years and when the Task Force travelled across the country, Canadians seem to agree young people need to be taught about money matters in school. Since this has become part of the national debate, provincial education ministries are looking at ways to get financial literacy into the classroom, but there are different views on how it should be done. Some administrators are of the view that a high school credit course is not necessary and that elements of financial literacy can be worked into the curriculum in grades two through 12 in courses like math, social studies and other programs. In my own experience I never learned about credit cards, mortgages or car loans when I was in high school. I did learn about Bunsen burners in chemistry and I can tell you the day I left high school I never used one again. I feel I could have benefited knowing about compound interest, how the stock market works or the difference between a fixed and variable mortgage.

In March 2011, a U.S. survey found that 82% of parents felt a course in personal finance should be a high school graduation requirement. Even 76% of young people between the ages of 18 and 24 felt the same. Interestingly, the wealthier the respondents were, the more likely they were to support the learning of money management in school. Education is a provincial matter; therefore, it's up to the provinces to decide how financial literacy should be included into the curriculum. British Columbia, Manitoba, Ontario and Nova Scotia all have elements of financial literacy included in their educational system, or are working to include it in the near future, but in my view more could be done. I feel there are more than enough topics to make up a high school course and, unlike using a Bunsen burner, the information you will use for the rest of your life. One issue that is a potential stumbling block is who will teach these financial courses? A teacher may be excellent in the field of history and science, but may not feel comfortable teaching a course on financial literacy. Training, new textbooks, course outlines and teaching modules may be required.

Some parents who want their children to gain financial knowledge are even sending them to millionaire camp! I attended *Camp Millionaire* held at Seneca College in Toronto in the summer of 2011. It was amazing to see the enthusiasm and thirst that young people had for financial information. *Camp Millionaire* is run by Jorge Ramos of the Toronto based company Financial Intelligence Inc. The program is for students nine to 14 years old, and promises to give them the tools they need to become the next Donald Trump—minus the bad hair. I asked Ramos if kids really want to spend a week at a summer camp talking about money matters instead of canoeing or riding horses. Ramos says, "These kids really do want to be here. There are some who say they were sent by their parents, but very quickly they see this is something they need to learn. Plus we make it fun, interactive and show them when they are in charge of their money it can help them fulfil their dreams." The camp focuses on what Ramos calls the three pillars of wealth; real estate, business and the stock market. As well as classroom instruction there is a field trip to a local business, a stock brokerage, real estate firm and a bank. Ramos says what he is teaching in his camp is what should be taught in the school system. He says, "It's not taught in school at all at this point and while they are looking at introducing it, many of the teachers that I've spoken to don't feel equipped to teach this material, which is why we have started working with school boards to see how it can be integrated."

The students I spoke with at *Camp Millionaire* seemed to be enjoying the experience and many could be future business titans to be reckoned with. Twelve year old Robert Manz told me he enjoys helping his mother with the family finances. Manz told me, "I can't wait to get rich. I want to be a big entrepreneur and build a financial empire." So you are going to be a millionaire, I asked him? "Yes, a millionaire for sure and maybe even a billionaire." I also met 12 year old Joseph Shlayen who said he was glad to be at the camp so he would learn to manage money wisely so he can be a millionaire when he grows up. He told me, "I personally would like to own many different companies. I also learned that the stock market is affected by many different things. It's not just if one company is doing better than another, stock prices could be affected by matters beyond anyone's control such as the weather, if planes are delayed or different events happening in the world." I asked Shalayen if he thought financial literacy should be taught as part of the regular school curriculum. He said, "I think it should be taught in school, but not in grade school because in grade school you need to learn the basics. In high school you have a choice of what you want to learn so I think it should be taught in high school or at least be an option for students who want to take it."

Two young girls attending *Camp Millionaire* also had an interesting perspective. Ava Lioutas told me, "I don't know if I want to go into finance in the future, but I believe it's really important to learn how to manage your money because it's something you can use for the rest of your life." Cindy Chin added, "I think it's good to learn about money and how it can lead to financial freedom, because then you can be successful in life."

Ramos goes a step further saying, "It's not just kids that need this information— it's parents too. I've had Moms and Dads come up to me after their kids have taken *Camp Millionaire* and say 'I wish I would have taken something like this when I was a kid.' In fact, I believe these basic lessons can really make a difference down the road and save a lot of marriages in Canada. So many divorces are caused by financial problems that I think I'm helping improve the marriage success rate in Canada." Maybe you are, Jorge. Ramos hopes to expand *Camp Millionaire* for next summer. For more information check www.financialiq.ca.

[5]
MONEY ADVICE
FROM YOUNG CANADIANS

Since this book is dedicated to helping Canada's youth be better with their finances, I thought it would be interesting to see what Canadian teenagers actually had to say about their first experiences with money management. Credit Canada has an annual essay contest for grade 12 students that asks the question, "What is the dumbest thing I have done with my money and what did I learn from it?" I got a chance to go through some 2010 contest entries and found three excellent essays I believe we can all learn from. Riviera Lev-Aviv from Thornhill, Ontario was the Grand Prize winner of $5,000 for her essay *The Lemonade Debacle of 2001*.

After her first attempt at entrepreneurship, Rivera realized there was no great demand for bouquets of dandelions so she decided the best plan of action was to construct an old fashioned lemonade stand with her three sisters. They pooled their resources, came up with $13.28 and made a trek to the grocery store for supplies. Once their homemade stand was set up, hand drawn signs were painted and neighbours began to show up and by the end of the day they managed to sell 13 glasses at 25 cents each. That's a grand total of $3.25. With her share from the profits of 81 cents, that evening Riviera spent the entire amount on candy. Riviera says, "I woke up the next day not only penniless, but in debt. It was time to declare piggy-bankruptcy." In hindsight, Riviera says the stand was doomed to fail as the lemonade cost more to make than they were selling it for. As she got older she took several jobs including positions as a barista, a cashier, a camp counsellor and a sales associate at a clothing store. It was when she worked at a 1970s themed burger

29

joint that she noticed something crucial that escaped her during the *Lemonade Debacle of 2001*. The restaurant actually charged more per beverage than it cost them to produce! Her next small business was more profitable. She combined her time with her mathematical expertise (no upfront capital required) and became a student tutor making $20 an hour. She deposits 75% of her pay into her bank account every week and leaves 25% for movies, mascara and candy. Riviera says she hopes to go through her first year of university debt free. She says "I have come to the conclusion that when life gives you lemons, you should make lemonade, enjoy some now, and put the rest in the fridge for another day."

Vivian Tam of Toronto won $3,000 for an excellent essay that shows how quickly you can spend money that has taken years to save. She wrote about a date that didn't turn out as planned in August 2010 in Toronto. "Lip gloss? Check. Mascara? Check. $120 blow dry, haircut and style from a top notch salon downtown? Check." Vivian says she looked and felt like a rock star and couldn't wait to arrive at a party that a cute guy she worked with had invited her to. However, as soon as she arrived dressed to impress and wearing the latest Italian footwear, instead of hearing dance music, she smelled oil, fries and ketchup. She says that's when she saw a 'Happy 5th Birthday' banner hung across the front porch and heard the shrieks of children. It was certainly not the party she was dressed for, and by the time she turned around to make a quick exit her $45 taxi ride was gone. Her date shouted, "This isn't exactly the party you were expecting, was it?"

Vivian goes on to recount how this one night caused her not only to blush five shades of embarrassment, it also wiped out a good chunk of her savings. It's a day she can thankfully look back on now with tears of laughter, but she will always remember the lesson she learned that day. Vivian says, "I realized runway fashions are not appropriate for everyday wear, no amount of makeup masks embarrassment, and that impulsive purchases can sometimes be the most unnecessary of expenditures." She added that, "My account balance of $1,900 in savings from many years of birthdays, Christmases and savings from my minimum wage job was reduced by $500 because of my one night of glamorous preparation. More than a third of my balance disappeared that I had saved for 16 years!" She says she was ashamed and embarrassed to tell her Mom about her reckless spending who was constantly reminding her how hard it is to earn and save money. Vivian says after this embarrassing incident, she keeps track of every purchase and makes sure it is a need and as opposed to one of her never ending wants. Vivian says "This experience taught me the very morals my parents emphasize every day—the value of money and the wisdom necessary to spend it well. I plan to pursue a Bachelor of Medical Sciences, and to leave undergraduate school debt-free." Vivian believes we learn from our mistakes and says even though her path to financial maturity cost her $500, it also provided her with the wake-up call she needed to take responsibility for her finances.

Andrew Darcovich from British Columbia won $1,000 for his essay on the perils of overspending. He remembers racing down the street on a new scooter with friends to get to the local corner store. He says, "I treated the whole gang to colas ($7), chips ($12), and over $30 in chocolate and candies!" Later that night it was coffee and dessert ($8) and a movie ($15). Andrew says at the age of 13 on the first day of summer he had already spent over $70! On day two, he was invited to the Pacific National Exhibition with a friend and another round of spending began. Andrew says, "Just to get in was $30 and then I spent dollar after dollar on outrageously priced hotdogs and sodas and to top it off I spent the last $40 I had on a ride called the Revelation, the scariest one in the amusement park."

When Andrew's parents picked him up and learned of his empty pockets, they told him it was time to get a job. Andrew says he was thrilled about the idea at first and the next day relaxed at home and watched TV all day. Doing this cost him $0. But before long he was out job hunting and landed a position mowing lawns and landscaping. Soon, he had a steady income and a whole new work ethic. He says, "As the summer progressed I worked hard and long hours and by August I had gone out with my friends only twice. I would work, come home and go to bed, then work, come home and go to bed. The vicious cycle repeated itself over and over again. I had a new mentality to save, save, save!" There were no more movies, candy runs or trips to amusement parks. His friend even began to call him "The Hermit." One day when he was cutting a lawn he noticed an old man walk by wearing an expensive watch, finely polished shoes, an impeccable suit, yet a sad face. As he cut the grass, the man sat down nearby and he could see that he was crying. Andrew says "I was shocked and went over to see if he was ok." That's when the man told Andrew that his wife had passed away a couple of years ago and he came to sit on the bench, the site of the first date, to remember her.

Throughout his 60-year marriage, the old man recounted how he spent all of his time working long hours trying to make money and become rich to the point where he barely saw his children or parents. They were all ignored in his pursuit of "happiness," not realizing at the time that true happiness was all about love, friends and family. It was at this point, Andrew says, he had a greater understanding of the value of money. "I had been at both ends of the money spectrum, spending every cent I had on unnecessary impulse purchases and then completely the reverse, clinging to every dollar I earned like a miser." Andrew says he learned from the old man that while money is important, it can't buy happiness which is why it's really all about balance. Andrew ended his essay saying he still balances his spending and saving and still occasionally sees the old man on the bench who he now knows as Bill, who is 94 years old. Andrews says, "We meet for lunch every once in a while, but which restaurant we go to depends on which one we have coupons for." Well done Andrew. Another great essay with an important message for all of us. Often it takes a life lesson to learn the hard way the right thing to do and these three young Canadians now appear to be on the right track.

[6]
SO WHO ARE THE CANADIAN MILLIONAIRES?

Canada currently has 60 individuals or families worth more than a billion dollars. Our richest Canadian is businessman David Kenneth Roy Thomson, son of Kenneth Thomson. (I met Kenneth Thomson once when I was doing a TV story and despite his enormous wealth, he was a very pleasant and down to earth man.) David Thomson is the Chairman of Thomson Reuters and he and his family are worth an estimated 23 billion dollars, making them the richest people in Canada and 17th richest in the world, according to *Forbes Magazine* in 2011.

Most of us believe that a billion dollars will never be within our grasp, but a million dollars certainly could be. If you think most millionaires inherited their wealth or had money handed to them by rich parents or relatives, a recent study found that is not the case. Research by BMO Financial Group in 2011 found that the vast majority of wealthy Canadians made their million dollars the old fashioned way—through hard work, saving and investing.

The study found that most Canadian millionaires were involved in professional activities such as doctors, lawyers and executives while the rest were the owners and operators of their own business. It also found that 94% of the 459 Canadians with at least $1 million in investable assets made it on their own with only 6% getting their hands on a million bucks through an inheritance. That's good news for the average Canadian because it shows even if you start out in life with nothing, a million dollars is a very achievable goal.

To be classified a millionaire, or high net worth individual (HNWI), you need to have at least 1 million dollars in investable assets. This does not include a house,

33

cottage or expensive Lamborghini sports car. It's a million bucks free and clear. Currently there are about 10 million millionaires in the world. About 375,000 live in Canada. The number fluctuates each year, but it's estimated that 40% of Canada's millionaires live in Ontario, 23% in Quebec, 16% in British Columbia and 12% in Alberta. So what do these millionaires have in common that we can learn from?

William Danko and Thomas Stanley wrote the ground breaking book, *The Millionaire Next Door* and they found that most millionaires became first generation rich by working hard, being careful with their money and not overspending. When they set out to interview millionaires, they originally went to affluent American neighbourhoods with extravagant homes, expensive luxury cars out front, and in-ground swimming pools in the back. They were shocked to find that many people living this lifestyle were not actually wealthy. They found many of the huge homes had huge mortgages, the luxury cars were leased and while the occupants had high salaries, they had no net worth. Instead they found millionaires in modest homes, working and living next door to people with a fraction of their wealth.

Instead of millionaires driving Porsches, wearing Rolex watches and dining out every night, their research showed many millionaires drove Ford pickup trucks, lived in their original homes and shopped at Sears and Wal-Mart. Through his research on millionaires, Danko has this advice for the rest of us, "Live on 80% of what you make. If you can systematically save and invest 20% of whatever you are making and let the time value of money work for you, you can't lose." He says too many people hope there will be a magic bullet to make them wealthy when he says it's really about buckling down and living on less.

Thane Stenner is known as Canada's "advisor to the wealthy" and along with being the managing director of Stenner Investment Partners, GMP Private Client L.P., he is also the author of *True Wealth; An Expert Guide for High Net Worth Individuals and Their Advisors*. Stenner says there are many things that young people can learn from the habits of Canadian millionaires. He says, "First and foremost they are not prone to overconsumption. In almost all cases they are ready to sacrifice something today in order to achieve greater wealth and prosperity in the future." Stenner adds, "There are lots of people who look wealthy. They drive fancy cars, they live in upscale homes and wear expensive suits but when you examine their true wealth—it's a different story." While many of Stenner's clients are business owners and entrepreneurs he says, "If someone is prudent with their wealth it's possible to use an average income to accumulate an above average net worth." If 80% to 94% of Canadians made their million on their own it shows it can be done. When these individuals do bank a million dollars it's not material stuff they crave. Research shows what they value most is safety, security and peace of mind. If you could have a million bucks in the bank, that would give you peace of mind, too. Later in this book we will look at ways to help make that happen.

[7]
SO YOU WANT TO BE A MILLIONAIRE— WHAT DOES IT TAKE?

A million dollars is often the magic number that many of us think would help make our lives easier. The truth is, a million dollars does not go as far as it used to, and many people would likely still need to continue to work even if they won a million dollars in a lottery (unless they were already relatively well off). In this earn and spend society, many people also believe the only way they could ever possibly have a million dollars is to win it. But the truth is, the possibility to save a million dollars in your pre-retirement lifetime can be done without too much trouble.

How is that? Well imagine saving 20 dollars a week—every week. Sure it may be hard to do in the beginning, but once you start setting aside 20 dollars a week, or 40 dollars every payday, it becomes habit forming. If that money was put into an investment such as a mutual fund which could be an Equity Fund, Balanced Fund or Dividend Fund that can be set up at any bank, then it will be ready to grow. Mutual funds are investments that hold shares in many different businesses and they are typically less volatile than owning individual stocks. They will fluctuate with the stock market but have been shown over time to go up. (We will talk more about mutual funds later in this book.) It's possible for a balanced fund which is fairly conservative (not too risky) to return 8% a year. For example, let's imagine we have invested in a fund that does better with a return of 10% annually. What would it do over time? Well if you put 20 bucks a week into a mutual fund that was able to generate an average annual return of 10% you could save your own jackpot! Look at the figures.

$20 a week x 52 weeks a year x 10 percent x 30 years = $206,329

$20 a week X 52 weeks a year x 10 percent x 40 years = $553,396

$20 a week x 52 weeks a year x 10 percent x 50 years = $1,453,598

Now I know you're saying I don't want to wait 50 years to have a million dollars and I don't blame you. There is also no guarantee of getting a 10% return every year as some years it may be higher, others lower. But what this shows is that saving even a little money can really add up overtime, especially with the magic of compound interest! (We are going to talk a lot about our friend compound interest later.) I'm not saying you shouldn't play the lottery occasionally if you want to try and win the big jackpot ($20 million would be nice), but watching your spending and saving as little as 20 dollars a week can help you save your own jackpot—just in case your lottery numbers don't come in.

[8]
ARE YOU A SPENDER OR A SAVER?

I met a young woman on maternity leave who said she had a good job with her pay topped up to 100% while she was home with her baby. She was pushing her daughter in a $500 stroller (one of three she said she owned). She said she went to the movies every week, dined out with her husband twice a week and had a maid come in every weekend to clean her house. She asked me if there was any way I knew she could make some extra money. Why I asked? "Because we are struggling. There is never enough money to go around." Of course this young woman didn't have an earning problem. She had a spending problem, but she just couldn't see it.

Many people are born to be great athletes, painters or singers. Some of us are also natural savers and many of us also seem like we were born to spend! Some of us even practice what's known as "Retail Therapy"—shopping to make ourselves feel better. I remember when we first gave an allowance to our two youngest daughters, one took her first ten dollars and put it in her bank account. The other took her ten dollars and bought a massive Toblerone chocolate bar! (I won't name which one to avoid any embarrassment—ok it was Vanessa.) The good thing is that if you can figure out what kind of person you are, you can work to overcome bad habits and make yourself a better saver.

Saving too much money is not a rampant problem these days, but there are people in extreme cases who may actually need to spend some money to enjoy life and have fun. When I was growing up I knew of two brothers who saved every nickel they ever made, but they had no social life, went nowhere and did nothing. That's not much of an existence as a fulfilled life is all about finding the right

37

balance. Currently it is overspending that is a huge problem with a large section of our population, and in our consumer driven society there are always tempting products, slick advertising campaigns and aggressive pitchman ready to try and part us from our hard earned money.

While Canadians have traditionally been better savers than Americans, that has recently changed and now Canadians have a debt-to-income ratio that is actually higher than Americans. In early 2011, the ratio of household debt-to-disposable income level reached its highest level ever at 148.1% according to Statistics Canada. (This means we are spending more than we earn, saving less and paying more for debt relative to our incomes.) This worries the Bank of Canada because if interest rates go up suddenly, and at some point they will, many Canadians won't be able to handle higher mortgage and loan payments. Bank of Canada Governor Mark Carney said, "We've seen a bit of deceleration in the rate of growth of consumer debt, but it's still growing faster than income." While it helps our economy when people spend money on goods and services, no one wants Canadians spending so far beyond their means that they are going to end up broke.

If you are a natural saver you are a very lucky person already. You may enjoy putting money away for a rainy day. You don't need the latest gadgets, fashion fads or trinkets. You like watching your bank account grow. You understand a used car may be as good as a new one. You don't feel the need to eat out in restaurants all the time. You think renting a movie and watching it at home can be just as much fun as going to the cinema. You know that by spending less than you make, you will get ahead day by day.

If you are a natural spender you will have to change your ways or you could be headed for a lifetime of debt and never be able to get ahead. That may sound like a dire warning, but it's true. As you get older there is nothing wrong with wanting to reward yourself with a vacation, a new flat screen TV, a new car and a meal at a nice restaurant. But natural spenders sometime want all of these things at once with no regard for the future and how much things cost. Spenders will then often use credit cards, lines of credit and bank loans to finance their spending lifestyle. This means they are then paying back interest on their debt as well. (Interest is the rate which is charged or paid for the use of money and, as you'll see later on, some credit cards have interest rates of 29.9%.) If you are paying interest on your debt and you don't change your spending ways, it will be very difficult to get ahead.

Often people think it may be the poor who get themselves into debt, but studies show that consumers from all walks of life can get into financial difficulty whether they are a chef, a mechanic or a doctor. There are people with six-figure incomes who need to seek credit counselling because they are spending more than they make. Whether you have a natural tenancy to spend or save, you can change yourself for the better. My daughter Vanessa who wanted the giant chocolate bar learned her lesson when the chocolate was gone and her sister Sarah still had ten dollars in the bank. Now Vanessa has become a very good saver. She asked if she could go on a humanitarian trip to Africa to help build a school, than added, "it's only $4,500." "Only?" I said. I decided I would pay for half the trip if she could somehow come up with the other half. So she immediately started handing out resumes and at 16 years old she is now the newest employee at our local pita shop. She is now putting every paycheque in the bank, saving up the other half of her trip to Tanzania. It is a great lesson for her and I hope it will help saving become a lifelong habit. I know she will enjoy the trip that much more because she had to work to help pay for it.

[9]
KNOWING WHAT YOU'RE WORTH

If you want to be in control of your finances you really need to keep track of where your money is going. The best way to know if you are getting ahead or falling behind is by knowing your financial worth. Calculating your financial worth is an exercise many successful people do on a monthly basis, or at least once a year, and it's easy to do. Just think what if you had to sell off everything you had and needed to pay off all of your debts—what would you be left with? It's subtracting your assets (what you own) from your liabilities (what you owe) to determine what you're worth.

As you get older you will have many different items to add to your financial worth calculation. Assets such as a home, stocks, RRSPs or a cottage. You'll also have liabilities such as a mortgage, car loan, credit cards, lines of credit, property taxes and other bills. Even if you don't have a lot of "stuff' in the early stages of your life it never hurts to see exactly where you stand financially.

Here's an example of a net worth calculation for 23 year old Samantha who just finished college and started her first job.

ASSETS	
Car	$6,800
Savings account	$2,300
Total Assets	**$9,100**

LIABILITIES	
Student Loan	$16,000
Car loan	$2,600
Credit Card Bill	$875
Total Liabilities	**$19,475**

Assets – Liabilities = Net Financial Worth
$9,100 – $19,475 = – $10,375

Yes, that's right, Samantha has a negative financial worth, but she shouldn't be alarmed as she is just starting out, has student loans to pay and just started her first job. Many younger people will begin their financial lives this way—with more debts than assets. That's just the way it goes. However, as you begin to pay down debt and build wealth, your financial worth will go up. You will also start to establish a good credit rating which is very important (we'll talk about that later). Let's stay positive and check in with Samantha three years later.

ASSETS	
Car	$4,000
Savings account	$12,775
Investments	$4,185
Total Assets	**$20,960**

LIABILITIES	
Student Loan	$4500
Car loan	$0
Credit Card Bill	$150
Total Liabilities	**$4,650**

Assets – Liabilities = Net Financial Worth
$20,960 – $4,650 = + $16,310

As you can see now Samantha's car is paid off, but worth less. She has managed to add to her savings account and even make her first investments (maybe in an RRSP or a Tax Free Savings Account we will talk about later). On the liabilities side, her student loan is down to $4,500, her car loan is finished and she now as a financial net worth of $16,310! Samantha also has good credit reputation with her bank and is viewed as a valued customer.

Keeping track of your financial worth is an important exercise because often when people don't realize what kind of financial shape they are in, they go on making the same mistakes year after year, not knowing they are not getting ahead and in fact, they may be falling behind. Let's face it, many of us spend 15 minutes trying to decide what movie we want to watch—so why not spend that much time once a month checking your financial position. You'll be glad you did, especially as you watch your net worth grow and your debts disappear.

[10]
WATCHING WHERE YOUR MONEY GOES

While it's important to know your financial worth to make sure you're always getting ahead, another important exercise is watching where all your money actually goes. It's hard to believe, but over a lifetime most of us will have a million dollars or more pass through our hands. That's a lot of money! The best way to tell if you are getting ahead is to write down your income and expenses—to see them in black and white. While your cash inflow is usually a set amount, there are always many different expenses that can quickly eat into your cash outflow if you're not careful. Let's take a look at 24 year old Colin who has been working for one year and rents an apartment in Ottawa.

February 2012

MONTHLY CASH INFLOW	
Colin's salary	$3,100
Other income	$0
Total Cash Inflow	**$3,100**

February 2012

MONTHLY CASH OUTFLOW	
Living Expenses	
Rent	$850
Utilities	$130
Cell phone	$65
Car insurance	$110
Tenant insurance	$30
Groceries	$240
Total Living Expenses	**$1,425**
Debt Payments	
Credit card	$130
Car loan	$350
Total Debt Payments	**$480**
Miscellaneous Expenses	
Gas	$100
Pick-up Hockey	$60
Vacation budget	$70
Dining out	$120
Movies	$40
Total Miscellaneous Expenses	**$290**
Total Cash Outflow	**$2,295**

Once you total these amounts, take your cash inflow, the amount of money coming in, and subtract the cash outflow, the amount of money going out determines whether you have a surplus or a deficit. In Colin's case it looks like this.

Cash Inflow – Cash Outflow = Surplus or Deficit
$3,100 – $2,295 = $805 Surplus

This exercise shows that Colin is in good shape each month and is able to have over $800 left to put in his savings account. He could start buying investments or saving for a down payment on a house or condominium. Of course this may have been a good month for Colin. Next month he could have an unexpected car repair, need to buy a new mattress or take an unexpected trip. This is an important exercise that can be performed every month to help you identify problem areas of spending. (If you're dropping $400 a month dining out, you might want to pack a lunch.)

To make this easy you can create one budget worksheet (leaving spaces for the amounts) and print off or photocopy 10 or 20 copies at a time that you can use over the course of the year. (Don't forget to save the budget worksheet on your computer so it's there when you need to make more copies.) Complete this exercise every month and keep them on file to help you monitor your expenses to make sure you are always in a surplus situation.

[11]
YOU ARE YOUR OWN SMALL BUSINESS

I was at a dinner party recently where a woman said she had a major dilemma. She had run up $20,000 in credit card bills and her husband didn't know about it. She felt worried, foolish and was unsure how to break the news to him, concerned it could lead to the end of their marriage because they were already having financial problems. Now I'm not sure that when he found out about the debt it ended their marriage, but I bet it did cause one heck of a fight. We all know about infidelity in a marriage when one partner cheats on their spouse with another person. Now there is a new kind of infidelity that is a growing problem—financial infidelity! This is when a husband secretly spends hundreds of dollars a month on poker, expensive custom-ized auto parts or electronic gadgets or when a wife may have a fetish for expensive shoes, handbags or designer fashions. Everyone should be able to treat themselves occasionally, but if you are spending thousands of dollars behind your partner's back, this kind of financial infidelity can be very damaging to a relationship.

The partner you choose in life is so important. Deciding to get married or live with someone should first and foremost be a matter of the heart, but it is also the biggest business decision you will ever make. Living with another person means you are making them a partner in your small business. There will be many different stages you will go through; buying a car, purchasing a home, taking trips, buying furniture, investing and saving for the future. If you and your partner are working together like a well-oiled machine, your small business will grow and flourish. If not, it can lead to a financial disaster for your business and unfortunately, many relationships end over problems with money.

If you are living on your own, then you are the CEO of your small business and are completely responsible for your household. If you are with another person, then you share the responsibility of spending and saving. All of us have money flowing in and out of our lives and if you manage it correctly, your small business will grow and flourish. If you don't, you could find your personal company in financial trouble or even worse—bankruptcy. This is why the relationship with your spouse is so important because together you will work as a team running your family business.

What good is it for a spouse to work overtime if the extra money earned is wasted on frivolous purchases? Why clip coupons and watch for sales if funds are blown on the latest expensive fashions. All the money-saving techniques and strategies are of little value if you are not working together as a couple heading in the same direction. It's always a good idea for both people in a relationship to know the financial situation of the small business. A small business checks its books often and does a year-end analysis and so should you. Are you getting ahead? Falling behind? Saving for the future or getting deeper in debt? Both people in the relationship should know what is going on. After all, would the co-owner of a company allow the other partner full access to the books without looking themself? If you are on the outside, find out exactly what is going on. If you are the bookkeeper, throw open the balance sheets to your spouse so they know the company's bottom line, whether it's good, bad or otherwise. Too many couples are running on a financial treadmill, paying off $450 in debt one month, but at the same time racking up another $500 in debt. It may feel like you are getting ahead, but when you look at the figures you can see that, in fact, you are not.

Unfortunately one of the main things couples fight about is money. So if you want to have peace in your home and your relationship on solid ground, treat your marriage like a company and your spouse like a partner. It's not always easy, but you should never be in denial about your finances. If you are currently having financial problems, don't bring up money issues in the heat of an argument. Set aside time in a non-confrontational way, such as by saying, "This weekend, let's talk about our finances. We could do it after dinner on Sunday night." In extreme cases you and your spouse may need counselling, but if that is what is needed to save your small business, then do it.

Consider these numbers of Canadian households, according to *2006 Canadian Census*:

- Number of Canadian households in Canada 12,437,500
- People living in family households 69.6%
- People living alone 26.8%
- People living with one or more unrelated persons 3.7%
- Average size of a household 2.5 people

- Proportion of married couples (with and without children) 68.6%
- Common-law families 15.5%
- Lone parent families 15.9%
- Same-sex couples 45,300 with 16.5% married and 83.5% common-law

[12]
BE COOL—STAY IN SCHOOL

It is advice that has been around for many years, but now is more important than ever—stay in school and get an education! If you go to college or university you will earn more money than someone who does not. It's really that simple. We are in a knowledge based economy and there is more demand for skilled workers with higher education levels. Sure there are people who are entrepreneurs who have success without an education, but statistics show that you are more likely to earn more money, have greater assets and be more comfortable in your retirement if you have a post-secondary education. It is estimated that a young person with a university degree will earn 1.3 million dollars more than a high school graduate over their lifetime.

Young Canadians have been seeing the benefits of additional education over the past few decades. According to Human Resources and Skills Development Canada, the benefits of post-secondary education include higher earnings and lower unemployment risks, both of which contribute to your financial security. In 1981 almost half of the Canadian population, 48%, didn't have a high school diploma. In 2001 the number of young people without a high school diploma dropped to 31%. Higher education translates into higher salaries. According to statistics gathered in 2000, those who finished high school earned on average $4,300 a year more than those who dropped out. Going beyond high school meant even greater earning potential. Someone with a trade or college diploma earned on average $7,200 more than a high school graduate. If you have a university degree, you would earn an annual average salary of $48,600, nearly double that of a high school graduate at $23,000 more. More than a decade later these salaries would be much higher, even double. The differences in earning power between those who did or did not finish high school, have a college diploma or university degree are huge, and they will only grow farther apart as salaries continue to rise.

A survey in 2005 on savings and assets also found that a higher education also paid dividends over a lifetime. Statistics show those who have completed high school had average net assets (their total worth) of $120,000. That's $27,000 more than those who did not finish high school. The average assets among trades and college graduates was $171,000 and for university graduates it was close to $240,000. This means not only does someone start off earning more money, but over a lifetime and the span of a career, higher education also means higher growth in earnings, usually peaking between the ages of 50 and 54. Those with a higher education also enjoyed a larger income during retirement. University graduates had a retirement income more than double that of someone with only a high school diploma.

A higher education also means it will be less likely that you will go through periods of unemployment or low income.

UNEMPLOYMENT RATE BY EDUCATION LEVEL 2006	
No Diploma	12.3%
Finished High School	6.5%
Trades or College Diploma	5.1%
University Degree	4.0%

Just these statistics alone should be enough to make most young people see the benefits of continuing on after high school so they can achieve higher salaries, earnings growth, lower job loss risk, greater accumulation of net worth, higher income in retirement, and less stress! Whenever I visit high schools I tell students to work hard and stay in school because it will pay off in the future and the numbers show that it's true.

PART TWO

[13]
REDUCING DEBT

In my last book, *The Smart Canadian's Guide to Saving Money*, I told readers to stop keeping up with the Joneses because the Joneses are broke. "Keeping up with the Joneses" is a phrase that sums up how we compare ourselves to our neighbours as a benchmark for our social standing or the accumulation of material goods. The expression actually comes from a comic strip in 1913 when a family is constantly trying to keep up with their neighbours, the Joneses. Almost 100 years later we are still trying to impress them! We want to show we are as successful as they are and anything they can buy, we can buy better. The problem is that if the Joneses are big spenders, we will feel the need to try and keep up with their luxury cars, in-ground pool, twice yearly vacations and weekly trips to expensive restaurants. Trying to keep up with the Joneses will ensure you stay broke. Worry about your own life and not your neighbours and you will be a lot happier, less stressed and have more money in your bank account.

[14]
BAD SPENDING HABITS

Old habits die hard and if you have an expensive vice it can be a drain on your bank account. For young women the temptation may be Gucci handbags, designer dresses or expensive shoes. A young man may want to look stylish in expensive clothes, buy pricey golf clubs or dine out too often. Either way, it's easier now than ever to be a big spender. There are some obvious bad habits that can burn a hole in your pocket. Smoking or excessive alcohol consumption is neither good for your physical or financial health. A pack of smokes a day at $9.50 a pack equals $3,467 a year. A case of 24 bottles of premium beer at $36 a week is $1,872 annually. The cost is about the same if you prefer two bottles of fancy wine every week. Everyone should be aware that excessive spending on fine jewellery, movie collections or the latest fashions can make saving money virtually impossible.

I know people who can't get through the day without having a $4 latte and a latte a day adds up to $1,460 a year. I know we are currently in the age of downloading music, but when I was younger I bought 8-tracks, albums, cassettes and finally CDs. I was so pleased to finally have a way to keep music for the long term (without scratches and stretched tape!). I used to buy one or two CDs a week. They were 20 bucks each at the time and even buying one CD a week adds up to more than $1,000 a year. I curtailed my music spending long ago and have to admit there are only about 20 in my large collection that I listen to now with any regularity.

The same can be said for DVD and video game collections. How many times do you really need to watch a movie? If you are a *Twilight* or *Avatar* fanatic or you want movies for young children, it can make sense to purchase films, but beginning a DVD collection is an expensive proposition. Another bad habit that can easily cost consumers thousands of dollars a year is excessive dining out. Brown bagging your lunch takes some getting used to, but over time it's a great thing to practice because not only will you save a lot of money, it's often healthier too. The same is true of expensive clothing. There is nothing wrong with having a nice wardrobe, especially if you need to look a certain way for your job, but it's easy to spend thousands of dollars trying to impress people and overspending on clothing can be a wasteful and reckless habit. Going to the movies or playing golf can be a great pastime, but just as an example, let's look at how quickly costs add up.

GOING TO THE MOVIES	
Tickets for two	$24
Popcorn and drinks	$12
Total	**$36**
Four movies per month for 12 months	**$1,728**

GOLFING	
Golfing for one	$68
Four times per month	$272
Over six months	**$1,632**

Unfortunately another bad habit that can also become a problem is gambling. Whether it's playing Texas Hold'em with friends on weekends or visiting a casino, it's very easy to have hundreds of dollars slip through your fingers in no time. An occasional card game or casino visit with friends may be fine, but gambling won't help your financial situation and even though you may get lucky occasionally, you'll never get ahead.

Ten Common Money Wasters

1. Dining out often at restaurants
2. Buying expensive clothing and jewellery
3. Using premium gasoline (if your car doesn't require it; most don't)
4. Dry cleaning clothes you could wash yourself
5. Buying a brand new car
6. Using name-brand products when generics will do
7. Flying first class
8. Running up excessive cell and phone bills
9. Purchasing extended warranty plans
10. Buying DVDs, CDs and computer games

[15]
GOOD DEBT VS. BAD DEBT, UNDERSTANDING LEVERAGE

Debt is something most of us have to have in order to function in today's society. Unless you are a very lucky young person, you will have many different things in life that will cause you to be in debt—student loans, credit cards, lines of credit and mortgages. Then there is also the fun stuff like trips to Punta Cana in the Dominican Republic, home theatre systems and hot tubs.

Quite simply there are two kinds of debt—good debt and bad debt. Good debt produces cash flow whereas bad debt doesn't. Bad debt is a loan for a depreciating asset such as an SUV, a motorcycle or a weekend in Las Vegas. Good debt is a loan to buy something that will usually grow in value such as your home, a cottage or investments. Buying a flat screen TV on a credit card is bad debt. Buying a three-unit apartment building to rent out has potential to be good debt. Borrowing money to go to school, take a professional training course or make an investment in yourself is also considered to be good debt. Bad debt is mostly a result of the endless temptation of dining out, movies, gifts, golf, vacations or other entertainment.

Life is all about balance and we all need to have some fun along the way, but if you can follow this one basic rule, you'll be on the road to financial independence.

If you are going to buy something that doesn't go up in value—pay cash for it.

This may be easier said than done and difficult to do if you are buying a car. That's why you should be careful not to spend too much on vehicles when you are still in the process of paying down debt. Recognizing the difference between good debt and bad debt is what helps many rich Canadians become richer. Not knowing the difference is what keeps poor Canadians poor. Leveraging is another important tool used by the wealthy to enhance their bottom line. Leveraging is basically "using other people's money—to make money." Most of us have our first experience with leveraging and good debt when we buy our first home. You borrow money to buy a house, it appreciates in value (usually and hopefully) and you get to live in it. It's a winning combination. For example, let's look at a buyer who has $25,000 to put down on a $275,000 home. If that home rises in price to $300,000 then that buyer has effectively doubled their money. They have turned 25,000 into $50,000! Over time, if the home rises $100,000 in value, then the buyer has turned his initial $25,000 into $100,000! This is the power of leverage—using the bank's money to increase your bottom line. At the same time you will be paying down your mortgage on your home and seeing your net worth increase. The power of leverage, combined with saving and paying down debt, can give you an astounding return on your money.

It's important to note that leveraging does not always have positive results. As mentioned, buying a home *for the long term* is generally considered to be good debt and a good example of leveraging because, hey, you have to live somewhere. However, if you buy a home and borrow $450,000 from the bank to pay for it and the housing market has a correction (a dip in real estate prices), you could be living in a home worth less than what you paid for it. We will talk more about this in the homes section and why you shouldn't stretch to get into a house that is more than you can afford.

Many investors who borrowed money to invest in the stock market learned the hard way that leveraging doesn't always have positive results, such as when the stock market crash of 2008 happened. They opened themselves up to greater losses because when their stock prices started going down, they had been investing with borrowed money. People not only lost up to 50% or more of their investments, they also had to continue to pay monthly interest payments on their losses and still pay back the original money they borrowed. The goal may be to borrow $60,000 in order to turn it into $120,000, but as you'll see in life there is usually no such thing as easy money and experienced investors will tell you the stock market can be a dangerous place to be. (We will address that later in this book as well.) Bottom line—leveraging must be used with caution and respect.

If you can educate yourself to know the difference between good debt and bad debt and the possible advantages and disadvantages of leveraging, you will be in much better shape to try and save for the future and manage your finances.

[16]
DEBT CONSOLIDATION—
WHY IT DOESN'T ALWAYS WORK

If you have high interest credit card debt, it can make sense to take out a consolidation loan at a lower interest rate. But is it always the best thing to do? Not necessarily and here is why. Many people who are constantly consolidating debt never get to the root cause of why they have so much debt in the first place, which is almost always overspending! It can be easy and even habit forming to move high interest credit card debt to a credit card with a lower interest rate, sometimes referred to as "credit card hopping." If you shuffle debt from one card to another or to a bank loan or line of credit, you won't get ahead. Consolidating various high interest rate balances into one, easy-to-handle payment is often just a quick fix. I call it rolling "junk debt" into a bigger pile. What is "junk debt"? It's what I call debt that has been rolled around so many times you can't remember what you originally went into debt to buy in the first place.

Credit counselling statistics show that more than 50% of consumers who consolidate credit card debt have equal or higher amounts of credit card debt within two years.

No wonder banks and credit card companies make it so easy for you to consolidate. Just because a banker will approve a consolidation loan for the maximum amount you qualify for doesn't mean you should accept it. You may also be tempted by low-rate introductory credit card offers that allow you to transfer balances to take advantage of lower interest rates. However, often these cards have time limits so if you don't pay off the balance it won't be long before you'll be paying huge interest charges again.

An example of junk debt in action would be if you had a hot date and spent $120 on your credit card to pay for a meal at a chic restaurant. Let's say you didn't pay off your credit card at the end of the month and have an ongoing balance of about $1,800. If your credit card has an interest rate of 19% and you are only making minimum monthly payments, after a year you would have paid an additional $22.80 for that meal. Even if it was a great meal, do you still want to be paying for it? If you don't buckle down and pay off your debt, you may still have the balance going into another year. You are now not only paying interest—you are paying interest on your interest and you still haven't paid for your dinner the year before! If you eventually decide you shouldn't be carrying a balance on your credit card and take out a consolidation loan with a lower interest rate, it could take you another three to four years to pay for that dinner! The loans officer may suggest consolidating other debts such as what you owe on a department store credit card, what was left of a car loan and that trip to Punta Cana, in the Dominican Republic you haven't quite paid for. If the consolidation loan is for 9% over four years, this means you'll pay another $14 a year over four years for that meal you digested long ago. I hope it was a great date because that meal will now cost you about double.

I am not against debt consolidation if someone is serious about paying down debt and taking advantage of a lower interest rate. However, everyone should be aware that consolidating is a short-term solution that, in the long run, can cost you plenty. The example could also have been a DVD movie that wasn't very good or a pair of shoes that you only wore twice. So use debt consolidation as a tool in your favour because the banks are betting against you that you will run up your credit cards again and be back to consolidate again in the future.

[17]
MONEY FOR A RAINY DAY— THE EMERGENCY FUND

I remember doing a story for *CTV News* several years ago when a Canadian airline went bankrupt without warning, leaving it's passengers in Cancun, Mexico stranded. Many Canadians may have thought this was a great idea. Hey another few days in Mexico in the middle of winter and a legitimate excuse to tell the boss— count me in! What became alarmingly clear however, was how many Canadians didn't have enough money to pay for their meals and additional hotel stay. Even when the tour company offered to repay the stranded tourists when they got home, some just didn't have the cash or the space on their credit cards for an additional three days stay. Some tourists complained loudly about their dilemma, but what it showed was that some people were willing to push their resources to the limit to take a vacation that included no margin of error because if something went wrong, the truth of the matter was—they were flat broke.

It's amazing how many families have joint incomes of $85,000 but still have great difficulty coming up with $400 for an unexpected expense. They may have to resort to cash advances on their credit cards, juggle bank accounts or, as the old saying goes, "rob Peter to pay Paul." I guess it's an old saying because it's a consumer behaviour that's been around a long time. If you are someone who takes a deep breath every time you use your debit or credit card hoping there is enough money left to cover your purchases, then you know you have to get your finances in order. It's no way to live and it's stressful, too. We need to try to have some money set aside for emergencies like when the stove needs a repair, the furnace breaks down or you need new brakes for the car. If we don't, we are sometimes forced into making bad financial decisions such as signing up for high interest rate credit cards or piling debt onto a line of credit.

One shouldn't be in constant worry they are going to get divorced, lose their job or be struck with a serious illness, but it's something you should occasionally consider. Having some money set aside for emergencies should be part of your total financial strategy. Some financial experts say you must have at least six months' salary saved up in case you lose your job or have an unforeseen emergency, but the truth is most of us don't. I don't have six months' salary in my savings account. With the interest rates most banks pay for savings accounts I believe there are better places to keep your money. If I really did need that much cash fast I could sell off some investments (outside my RRSP and TFSA—we will talk more about that later) or use my line of credit if I needed a large amount of money in a hurry. Hopefully I won't have to resort to that and you won't either.

Here is the main problem with emergency funds; most of us struggle with what exactly an emergency is. A sale on hot tubs is not an emergency, nor is an opportunity for a last-minute trip to Los Angeles to tour wine country with your friends. It comes back to the whole "want or need thing" and it's human nature to spend easily accessible money and that can be a drawback to having six months' salary sitting in your bank account. You could have a bad week at the office and decide what you really need to unwind is a trip to Australia that just can't wait. Sure it would be fun but it's not an emergency. An emergency fund can be a true test of your willpower and discipline.

Home equity loans, cash advances on credit cards, and bank overdrafts are not emergency funds. If your backup plan is to dig yourself further into debt using more credit, then you really don't have an emergency fund. Do you really want to ask your parents for money? I wouldn't. That can also lead to all other kinds of awkward problems down the road. You should definitely try to have at least $3,000 to $5,000 in the bank so you will not be forced to turn to credit when the inevitable emergency comes knocking. The money should be easily accessible in your bank account, but depending on your willpower it may need to be set aside in a separate account from your debit and chequing accounts so you won't consider a Friday night concert an emergency. If you dip into your emergency fund for an unexpected legitimate expense, top it back up as soon as you can so the fund will be ready for your next rainy day.

As I mentioned, we will talk more about RRSPs and TFSAs (investments that can save you money on your taxes) later in this book. But keep in mind if you do put $10,000 in an RRSP and then decide to take that money out later because you have an "emergency", you will take a massive tax hit. When you put money in an RRSP the government gives you back money at tax time. If you decide to use your RRSP as an emergency fund and take the cash out—Ottawa will want the tax break it gave you back. Depending on your tax bracket, you could remove $10,000 and have to pay $4,000 back. So never count on using your RRSP as an emergency fund because it will be a costly mistake.

Bottom line? Keep some money in an emergency fund and try to think of where you could have a larger amount of money that you could get at in case you really did have an emergency. You'll be glad you did if that emergency does come knocking.

[18]
PAYING OFF STUDENT LOANS

These days student debt is a fact of life. Unless you have been fortunate enough to have help from your parents or other sources with your tuition, lodging and other school related bills, chances are you will graduate with a pile of student debt. A 2010 Statistics Canada report found the number of students who graduate with debt has risen over the past ten years from 49% to 57%. While students used to average about $15,000 dollars when graduation ceremonies wrapped up, that figure is now $18,800. While this can seem depressing, an investment in your education is one of the best moves you can make and you should never feel guilty about taking on debt to go to school. If you have chosen the proper career for yourself, your degree or diploma will more than pay for itself in your lifetime.

If you still have to go to university or college, are already there or have graduated, there will be different aspects of student debt you will need to be concerned about. One problem is that many students don't think enough about the incredible debt loads they are taking on while in school. If the average is almost $20,000, it means some students have $35,000 to $40,000 or more. As with any loan, money is easy to borrow and hard to pay back. If you are a full time student when you graduate from school or stop going, you will have a six month grace period on your loan before you have to start making payments. While this can help you get established, the important thing to recognize is that interest starts to accrue (accumulate) as soon as you take off your graduation sash. Deciding when you will start to pay off your student loan will most likely be affected by how soon you can land a job, hopefully in your chosen field.

There is a website that can help you determine how much your monthly student loan payment will be and how quickly you will be able to pay it off. The Loan Repayment Estimator at www.canlearn.ca is a helpful tool that can help you estimate the monthly payments you'll need to repay your student loan. Just fill in the information at the following link: tools.canlearn.ca/cslgs-scpse/cln-cln/40/crp-lrc/af.nlindex-eng.do

You can use the Loan Repayment Estimator before you go to school, while in school or after you have graduated to help you plan your monthly payments. It can feel like a heavy load to graduate from school with debt, but once you have your diploma or degree, the first thing you want to do is put it to work. If you are able to get a job in your chosen field, it will get you on the way to paying off your debts and building wealth for the future. You'll want to search for a job immediately, negotiate your salary carefully and set a timeline for when you hope to have your student loan paid back.

One mistake that many students make when they finish school is going on a spending spree and loading up on even more debt. They may feel a sense of entitlement or that they can afford it as they have finally joined the working world. I remember as a young journalist when I moved on from my first job, I was replaced by another young reporter. It was his first job and he went out immediately and bought all new furniture with "no money down" for his apartment. Unfortunately, he didn't make it through his three month probation so he was stuck with no job, a bunch of expensive furniture and he still had to pay for his student loans. Good advice to follow when you finish school and have debt—continue living like a student until your student loans are repaid. It's not that hard to do because you have already been doing it for two, three or four years. Some students let their student loan payments drag on forever, but believe me the sooner you pay off your loans, the better you will feel about it.

At tax time you should see if you are eligible for tax breaks because you are a student or are repaying student loans. The most common types of tax breaks for students include deductions or credits for tuition, textbooks, interest paid on student loans, moving expenses, child care expenses and public transit passes. So while you are a student, keep your receipts. If you missed these deductions, include them in your next tax return.

If you can't find a job or are having difficulty paying off your student loans there is help available.

- **Repayment Assistance Plan**—Helps you pay back what you can reasonably afford.
- **Repayment Assistance Plan for Borrowers with a Permanent Disability**—Helps borrowers with a permanent disability pay back what they can reasonably afford.

- **Permanent Disability Benefit**—If you have a severe permanent disability, you may be eligible to have your loans forgiven through the Permanent Disability Benefit program.
- **Revision of Terms**—You can ask to decrease or increase your student loan payments if you are having difficulty repaying your student loan debt or you wish to pay off your loan debt more quickly.
- **Canada Student Loan rehabilitation**—If your Canada Student Loan is in collection, getting it back on track may be easier than you think. If you have missed payments for more than 270 days and your loan is in collection, help is available. Check www.canlearn.ca for information on all these programs.

[19]
TRYING TO GET
A SCHOLARSHIP

College or university is expensive, so landing a scholarship is a real bonus. Even if your marks are more towards the middle of the pack rather than the top of the class, you can still get a scholarship for a wide variety of reasons. There is even one for being tall. There are many scholarships that don't have anything to do with marks, which is why every student should apply to see if they are eligible for some free money. The problem is many students don't know where to look, but now there is a helpful website that makes it easy; www.studentawards.com was established in 1998. It's a free scholarship matching service devoted to helping Canadian high school, college and university students find out information about scholarships, bursaries, grants, fellowships and other forms of financial assistance. Lesley Gouldie is the Chief Executive Officer of studentawards.com and says, "Our powerful search engine matches members with scholarships, bursaries and cash prizes, delivering customized lists of awards based on profile information that members provide when they register at the site. Our up to date national and bilingual database contains over $70 million in available awards, including hard-to-find and institutional prizes." Again, an interesting fact about scholarships is that less than half of the scholarships in the database are merit-based. That means even if you are not a stellar student with marks in the 90s, you still may be eligible to receive money to help pay for your schooling. Gouldie says, "Most scholarships are based on a number of varying criteria. Some do not judge based on marks at all while some place a very heavy weighting on marks."

Two million students have registered at the websites since 1998. Scholarships, bursaries and cash prizes are awarded from a variety of sources. They may come from private companies, banks, financial companies, universities, colleges as well as government institutions. Gouldie says, "Scholarships that are available vary in eligibility from part-time college student, to graduate medical student, even to mature students. There are scholarships available for both undergrad and graduate programs, to both college and university. Some scholarships are specific to a university or major, while others are open to all those who wish to apply regardless of degree or area of study." Some of the scholarships are for playing minor hockey, being tall or volunteering. There are also contests and cash prizes available to all registered studentawards.com members that sign up at the website. Goldie says, "Studentawards.com has given away close to $1 million to students to fund their education since the company was founded. These contests have included a video contest to best represent 'campus living' or a contest where students posted their 'New School Year Resolutions' online."

The best way to find scholarships on the Studentawards.com website is to fill out your personal profile so you can be matched accurately with all the scholarships hosted on the site. It's important to keep your profile updated so that you continue to receive accurate and current results on your scholarships search or you could be receiving information on med school scholarships when you've switched your degree to law. Also, make sure to check the emails you get from Studentawards. com notifying you of a new scholarship or an impending deadline and check the website often for the newest offers and contests that you might not get information about in an email. Some scholarships are specifically designed for employees of a certain organization, such as Tim Hortons while others may be solely available to recent immigrants, or relatives of war veterans. Gouldie says, "The criteria is wide ranging and astonishing, which is why we encourage students to register and fill out their profile as comprehensively as possible, to get the list of awards that pertain to them." There are also scholarships and cash prizes that are open to everyone seeking funding for post-secondary education. They may be essay questions asking a student how they would make their school more environmentally friendly, what they wish to accomplish with their degree, or best new ideas on how to improve an aspect of a certain company that is hosting the scholarship. I asked Goldie what was the best advice she could give a young person hoping to get a scholarship. She said, "Apply, apply, apply. The more you apply for, the more likely you are to win. Also, if a scholarship asks for references, make sure these references can be contacted when the time comes. This means current phone and email addresses. It's very difficult to consider an application seriously if no useable contact information is provided for references." Gouldie says it's also very important to follow the guidelines outlined for each scholarship, bursary or contest. If there is a rule about entrance videos being under five minutes, it has to be less than five minutes. If it goes over by a second it's ineligible. Same goes with word count. Most essay question response fields have an automatic cut off at the selected word limit, so if your essay question has a limit of 500 words, but you write 600, it is automatically chopped off at 500 and submitted to the judge that way."

So if you are attending post-secondary school and are looking for free cash, check out www.studentawards.com. The website also has help advice and information on student life, living in residence, finding a job, choosing a school, preparing a resume, saving money and even course selection.

PART THREE

[20]
DROWNING IN DEBT—
USING CREDIT RESPONSIBLY

In June of 2011 a study by the Certified General Accountants Association of Canada found Canadian households are drowning in an all-time high of $1.5 trillion worth of debt! If household debt was spread evenly among all Canadians, a family with two children would owe an estimated $176,461. Even more shocking, the survey found more Canadians are carrying debt into retirement, with one-third of retired households carrying debts of $60,000 into their golden years. Seventeen percent of retirees had debts of $100,000 or more. The report also found while Canadians were saving 18% of their disposable income 30 years ago, now on average Canadians are saving just 4.5%.

Fifty-seven percent of those asked said daily living expenses are the main cause of their increasing debt. Debt-to-income ratio in households reached a record high of 146.9% in the first quarter of 2011, compared to 144 % in late 2009. This means people owe more money than they are making, therefore getting caught in a spiral of debt.

In 2009, Statistics Canada conducted the Canadian Survey on Financial Capability. Here are some of their findings which the Federal Task Force on Financial Literacy used to help develop a National Strategy:
- 69% of Canadians have never requested a credit report
- 57% don't seek out financial advice
- 30% are not planning at all for their retirement
- 49% have no household budget
- 31% of Canadians are struggling to keep up with the bills

- 48% of Canadians planning to purchase a home saved less than 5% while 67% have saved less than 10%.

No one knows more about the problems facing Canadians when it comes to mounting debt problems than Laurie Campbell, the Executive Director of Credit Canada. I have interviewed Campbell many times over the years about financial issues facing Canadians and was also proud to serve with her on the Federal Task Force on Financial Literacy. Campbell says, "Parents are not talking to teens about money as much as they should be and, surprisingly, teens want to learn. They feel their parents are really missing the boat in speaking with them about financial issues." Unfortunately, debt loads are increasing every year for the vast majority of Canadians and it is becoming an even more significant problem. According to Campbell, "There doesn't seem to be a slowing down of people incurring debt. Interest rates have been low and the economy is bouncing back slightly, so people are living in a bubble believing that things are good, but I can tell you when interest rates start to go up, many people will be in big trouble. This could happen in 2012 and even an increase of a half of a percentage point will have a significant impact on how Canadians service their debt."

So who is coming through Campbell's door seeking credit counselling? She says it's a myriad of people from all walks of life, but adds, "There is no doubt that young people with student loans and credit card debts continue to be a big problem. On the flip side we're also seeing more elderly people. It's sad as now more people are retiring with mortgages and going into retirement with increased debt and a decrease in income which is clearly problematic." Campbell says another reason Canadian seniors are hurting is that many have been trying to help their children who had lost jobs, ended up in significant debt themselves or are going through separation or divorce. "At their own peril they are trying to help their children out," she says. Credit cards continue to be the biggest problem for Canadians having financial issues. Campbell says, "Impulse purchases with credit cards are huge. Credit cards are easy to get and interest rates are so high that people don't realize how quickly it can create problems. Some department store cards are now 29.9% and if you are only making the minimum monthly payments, it's almost impossible to get ahead."

So who is it that decides to go to credit counselling? Campbell says, "By the time people come to us, they want to turn their situation around; they want resolution. About 50% of the people who come to us are able to do that with a lot of management, financial coaching and budgeting. Actually, people like it better when we call it a spending plan rather than a budget, but we will call it whatever they like if it will help resolve their situation." You should know that anyone can go to a credit councillor to get budgeting advice or have a money management session. Campbell says, "It's part of our service because it's also about debt prevention.

Not for profit credit counselling services are coast to coast and free of charge. If you don't know how to manage your money and you're afraid of what your future looks like, then get counselling as we have financial coaches who can talk to you about your goals. We can help you build a strong financial future and avoid debt problems." If you are concerned about going to a credit counselling agency because it could affect your credit rating, Campbell says don't be. She says, "Just talking to a credit counselling organization means there is absolutely no record of it at all. The only time it would show on your credit report is if you'd have to have a third party intervention like a credit counselling service negotiate your debt on your behalf. This is only if the situation is severe enough and you don't have any other options." If you are in dire straits, one resolution is freezing your debt and stopping interest from accumulating, but Campbell says this "should not be viewed as a get out of jail free card, because there are consequences to having your debt frozen. It will show up on your credit rating that you had to have a third party intervention because you cannot handle repaying your debts on your own. You should really try to get out of debt yourself, but if you can't and really are struggling and need payments reduced and interest stopped, then that's what we are here for."

If you get credit counselling help, it stays on your credit rating for two years from the date of paying off your debts. Bankruptcy (the legal process that declares a person or business to be insolvent when a person or business can no longer pay their debts—more about that coming up) should only be considered as an opportunity of last resort, because it's really a financial death. Another area to be careful of that people get themselves in trouble over is co-signing loans. I get calls at CTV all the time from girlfriends who have co-signed loans for boyfriends who have then broken up, or parents who have co-signed for children who will no longer make the payments. Then you are completely liable to repay their debt. Campbell says, "Be very careful co-signing a loan for someone. Not only can it ruin your finances, it can also ruin relationships. My advice is don't co-sign. When you co-sign a loan you are fully responsible for that debt; you are responsible just like the original borrower." She also warns to be careful thinking that a debt settlement company can get you out of debt faster. Campbell says these for profit companies often tell people to try and save up enough money to try and pay a portion of their debt, but she says, "Many people don't have 20% or 30% to pay out a $40,000 debt. What these debt settlement companies will often tell you is to not pay any of your creditors for six months and to save up that amount and then they will pitch an offer to them. It's a dangerous game and you could have your wages garnished, lose any assets you may have and your credit rating will be destroyed. I would tell people to be very wary of any organization that offers this service."

I used this quote from Campbell at the beginning of this book and it bears repeating. When you are young and starting out, "It's like a clean slate, an empty page, and an opportunity to start out right. People don't realize that your finances impact you for your whole life; they impact your health, your relations, your work environment, and they can create addiction problems. So I say to young people, take it seriously. If you don't, the consequences are huge, way beyond your money." Well said.

[21]
CHOOSING THE RIGHT CREDIT CARD

When it comes to having too much debt, the major problem for the vast majority of young people is credit cards. They are so easy to sign up for and so hard for many people to use responsibly. Often it's the first financial instrument a young person gets that allows them to spend money they don't have. Credit cards make it very easy to run up bills but very hard to pay them back. Some consumer advocates want you to get out the scissors and cut up every credit card in your wallet, but the truth is most of us need a credit card to function in today's society. To book a hotel room, rent a car or shop online, a credit card has become a necessity. The best thing to do is to have the right credit card for your lifestyle and most of all—to pay it off every month!

The amount varies from year to year, but about 35% of all Canadians don't pay off their credit card balance every month. The Financial Consumer Agency of Canada also says that an amazing number of us, about 40% don't even know the interest rate we are paying on the credit cards in our wallets. For a news report, I once had to stop people on the street and ask them how many credit cards they had in their wallet. One woman told me she had 11! She said she needed them all because if she couldn't pay one credit card bill, she could use another credit card to pay it off. Not a good situation, just a continuing debt spiral. Too many people are concerned about reward programs, point plans and air mile offers to think about credit cards objectively. I did another story for CTV where we examined points cards and found with one gas station loyalty card you had to spend $11,000 on gasoline to get a $25 gas card! If people knew these figures they may not be so loyal.

There are credit cards that promise free trips, free groceries and free hotel stays, and these credit cards can be an excellent way to get free stuff, but it's only free if you pay off your balance every month. Make only the minimum monthly payment or miss a payment and the interest will quickly eat up any savings you may see. An example of a credit card that illustrates this very well is the card that allows you to save "two cents a litre" every time you buy gas. What a great idea as it keeps the customer loyal and saves them money.

Fill up once a week—60 litres of gas at $1.28 instead of $1.30 = savings of $1.20

Fill up 52 weeks a year x $1.20 = savings of $62.40

Maybe you expected more but at least it's a free tank of gas once a year.

However, this is only if you paid off your balance every month.

If you carried $1,000 on that credit card at 19% interest…$1,000 x 19% = $190.00 in annual interest charges.

So much for that free tank of gas.

The same is true of credit cards that reward you with air miles, hotel rooms or vacuum cleaners. If you pay off your balance every month you may eventually "earn" free stuff. If you don't, that free stuff will cost you plenty in interest charges. If you feel you have no choice but to occasionally carry a balance, see if you can qualify for a low interest credit card offered by most major banks. You may have to pay an annual fee of $20 to $45 but it may be worth it until you can afford to pay off your bill in full every month.

Credit Card	Balance on Card	Interest Rate	Annual Interest Charges
Low-rate card	$3,000	10.5%	$315
Major credit card	$3,000	19.0%	$570
Department store card	$3,000	29.9%	$897

The Financial Consumer Agency of Canada has a website that can help you chose the right credit card. With hundreds of different ones to choose from and each offering a different combination of interest rates, fees, benefits and rewards, it can help you research to see which one might be best for your lifestyle and budget. www.fcac-acfc.gc.ca

Creditcards.com is another website with a list of all Canadian credit cards from leading banks and financial institutions. It allows you to compare credit cards side by side. www.creditcards.ca

Review your credit cards annually to see if they are still the best choice for you, pay off the balance every month and remember, one to two credit cards is all you really need to function, even in our credit crazy society.

[22]
LINES OF CREDIT—
IT'S NOT YOUR MONEY!

First and foremost it is credit cards that continue to be the biggest debt obstacle for young people. As you get older and have your first home you may have to deal with something that could also be potentially hazardous to your wealth—the credit line. If you have a home and you have either paid off a portion of the mortgage or it has gone up in value, you may be offered a line of credit. A line of credit or credit line is an arrangement in which a bank or other lender extends a specified amount of unsecured or secured credit to a borrower. If your house is worth $250,000 but you only owe $150,000 on it, the bank may decide to arrange for you a $50,000 line of credit. The problem is that a line of credit is really just a giant credit card and some people make horrific financial mistakes with them.

According to credit rating agency TransUnion, lines of credit are now the largest category of consumer debt in Canada (excluding mortgages), accounting for more than 41% of the outstanding debt in Canada in 2011. Alberta and Ontario residents are the largest users of lines of credit, accounting for over 57% of their debt. Banks often push lines of credit as a great way to consolidate debt with a lower interest rate or a way to finance home renovations. When some Canadians start renovating though, they can't stop and the line of credit is an easy place to go to finance new bathrooms and basement projects.

The main issue with lines of credit is discipline. All of a sudden you have $50,000 in the bank and it feels like it's your money. But it's not; it's the banks. I remember when a man called me at CTV to complain that he had arranged a line of credit for $80,000 with his bank. He bought himself a van for $40,000 and decided to get one for his daughter for another $40,000. He was shocked to know the bank actually wanted the money back with interest! Make no mistake, a line of credit is just a loan. Some financial experts may argue that you should never have a line of credit, but the truth is they can be a handy way to have a certain amount of money ready for you to use, but only if you have a good reason to use it. Topping up your RRSP at tax time could be a good reason. Going on a trip to Las Vegas with friends is not. The main issue with lines of credit lies with human nature and our love of spending. Some of us can't resist the temptation when we see a credit line statement showing just how much we have available to spend. We break down and go on a shopping spree.

David Chilton, author of *The Wealthy Barber*, told me, "As I sit down and look at the financial plans of many Canadians, one of the things that jumps out at me that is very troubling is the aggressive use of lines of credit that has come into play in the last ten years. Way too many people are borrowing excessively on lines of credit and it is allowing them to live beyond their means! They rationalize that it's a low interest rate. So what! You still have to pay that money back. In fact, it's that rationalization that led to the abuse." Many people are using lines of credit to maintain a high lifestyle. Chilton says, "People believe their real estate will always increase in value. Well, the two are not as closely connected as you might think and nothing lasts forever—real estate can plateau. I actually think the banks have been too aggressive in pushing them. On occasion they can be a prudent move and a prudent planning technique, but for the most part they are to be avoided."

Bankers will often look at your financial situation and give you the largest line of credit your financial situation allows, but it doesn't mean you have to take it. If they offer you $50,000, just take $10,000. When you dip into your line of credit try to pay it back as you would any other bill. If you are signing up for a line of credit, you should ask yourself why are you getting it? What do you plan to use it for and do you even really need it? Never forget that a line of credit is just a credit card. It's just one you don't keep in your wallet.

[23]
MINIMUM MONTHLY PAYMENTS—BEWARE

The minimum monthly payment trap is very easy to fall into and many young people do. When I got my first credit card at 19 years old, I felt like I was officially an adult! I remember thinking I could go on a spending spree at a moment's notice because now I could "get it on credit." I knew at the time it was important to pay off the balance in full every month, but I assumed like most young people that as long as I was paying the minimum monthly payment each month, I was getting ahead. Well that's not the case and over time it's a very expensive mistake to make.

There has been such confusion over the years regarding the minimum monthly payment issue, that the federal government stepped in to make credit card companies spell out exactly how much it costs consumers if they don't pay off their balance every month. New rules mean credit card statements must now show the estimated time required to pay off your account if only minimum payments are made. The Financial Consumer Agency of Canada has an online calculator (www.fcac-acfc.gc.ca) that shows this and the time required can be quite a shocker. Here's an example:

Amy has an outstanding balance of $2,000.00 on a credit card with an 18% interest rate. Her minimum payment is $10.00 or 2% of the balance, whichever is greater. Amy's minimum payment would initially be $40.00 (2% of $2,000.00).

- If Amy makes only the minimum monthly payment of $40.00 every month, it would take her 30 years and 10 months to pay off her balance in full and she would end up paying $4,931.11 in interest.

- If Amy were to increase her monthly payment to $100.00, she would take only two years to pay off the balance in full and she would pay only $395.65 in interest.

It shows how expensive it is to pay only the minimum monthly payment and how increasing the monthly payment by even a small amount can drastically shorten the length of time it takes to pay off a credit card balance. The new rule forcing credit card companies to show this information was long overdue and has many Canadians seeing they may need credit counselling. Laurie Campbell with Credit Canada says, "We have clients coming in saying 'when I saw this I realized I can't get anywhere as it's going to take me 99 years to pay this off!' I think there's certainly more of awareness now, but good luck finding it on your statement. It's often buried in the fine print, not front and centre where it needs to be."

Another problem is that the minimum payment required has gone down over the years. Campbell says, "When I first started at Credit Canada 20 years ago, the minimum monthly payment was 5%, now it's only 2% for some credit cards. This can create an endless cycle of people paying the minimum monthly payment and never getting ahead. It is still very important to make at least the minimum monthly payment every month before the due date because if you don't, it could affect your credit score. Now that you know this information, make sure you never get caught in the minimum monthly payment trap.

[24]
YOUR CREDIT SCORE—
THE MOST IMPORTANT NUMBER

There is an old Bob Seger song I don't expect the younger generation to know, but it really sums up what it is like to be a consumer in the modern age. Seger recognized in 1978 how people were being treated by banks, utility companies and other financial institutions when he wrote the song *Feel Like a Number*. Here is a sample of the lyrics…

> *"I work my back till it's racked with pain*
> *The boss can't even recall my name*
> *I feel like just another*
> *Spoke in a great big wheel*
> *Like a tiny blade of grass*
> *In a great big field*
> *I'm just another statistic on a sheet*
> *I feel like a number"*

The truth is, every one of us is assigned a very important number that will follow us around for the rest of our lives and determine whether banks will lend us money, if we can be issued credit cards and it can even affect the amount we will pay for home insurance. It's called your Credit Score and big brother at Equifax and TransUnion, Canada's two major credit agencies, are watching your every financial move. They know every time we sign up for a loan, lease a car or get a department store credit card.

All of us have a credit rating, and that is really just our history of financial trans-actions. Your credit score is made up of a number of factors and you are judged on a sliding scale between 900 and 300. The higher your number, the better you are as a credit risk. When you borrow money, do you pay it back on time? If you have a cell phone, do you pay your bill every month? If you took out a car loan, did you make the payments without defaulting? If you always pay your bills on time and pay the money you owe, then you don't need to worry; your credit score will be fine. It will be a high number telling banks and other lenders that you are a good credit "risk" and likely to be a good customer in the future. But if you skipped payments, owe money and have not met your financial obligations, then you could have a low credit score which could cause you problems when you need to get a car loan or a mortgage.

Anyone can get their credit rating for free but you have to send away for it in the mail which can be a bit of a hassle (I'll tell you how shortly). To instantly get your credit rating and credit score you can do it online, but you'll have to pay a fee. To arrive at the magic number of whether you are a good credit risk is a mathematical calculation known as a FICO score that uses information in your credit history to determine the likelihood of whether or not you'll skip out on a car payment or miss a mortgage payment. FICO stands for Fair Isaac Company, the organization that developed the scoring mechanism for the credit score. In order to have a FICO score, you must have at least one open account on your credit report and that account needs to have been open for at least six months.

Most people don't know their FICO score, but you should because if you have a high score (the favourable end of the chart), you can use it to your advantage to try to get lower interest rates on loans. It doesn't hurt to find out if you have a low score either, because then you can work to improve it (remember it's between 300 and 900). Let's take a look at a FICO Score for Andrew Johnston.

Andrew has a FICO score of 780

So why did Andrew get a FICO score of 780? Credit agencies judge credit scores based on the following criteria:

- 35% of your score is based on your payment history. Have you paid your bills on time? How many have been paid late? Have you ever had a collection agency after you? Have you ever declared bankruptcy? How long ago these things happened will also affect your score. Something that happened six years ago will not impact your score as negatively as if you skipped a bill last month.

- 30% of your credit score is based on your outstanding debt. Are you swamped with debt already and have little room left to pay your bills? How much do you owe on your home and your car? How many credit cards do you have and are they at their limits? The more credit cards you have, again, the lower your score.

- 15% of your score is based on how long you have had credit. The longer, the better. Your past payment history can help predict how you'll pay your bills in the future.
- 10% of your score is based on the number of inquiries on your report. If you check on your own, that's not a problem. However, if there have been a number of inquiries from potential creditors, it may indicate that you've been all over town trying to get credit and have been turned down, so this will reflect poorly and lower your credit score.
- 10% of the score is based on the type of credit you already have; the number of credit cards along with outstanding loans. There is no perfect number that you should or shouldn't have, but this will be more closely scrutinized if there isn't an abundance of other information on your credit file.

The vast majority of us, about 70%, have credit scores between 700 and 850, which is an acceptable range to be in. Most lenders would consider offering you attractive interest rates and provide you with near instant approval. If your credit score is higher than 850, you are in the top five percent of the country with a select group of consumers who have an impeccable credit rating. If you are below 700, your credit rating is on shakier ground. If you are below 600, you may be turned down for loans and credit cards and should start working to turn around your credit score. The lowest category, which has credit scores between 300 and 500, has delinquency rates of 78%! Anyone in this zone will have a tough time getting credit of any kind.

One of the best ways to improve your credit score is to stop borrowing money! Only apply for credit when you really need it. Avoid signing up for new credit cards and maxing out the ones you already have. Remember every time you're late paying a bill, it's a black mark on your record. Your credit report also tells lenders if you have ever declared bankruptcy or co-signed for a loan, as well as your personal information, such as date of birth, addresses, employment information, creditors, payment history and inquiries that have been made into your credit history. You should know that all credit information, good or bad, is kept on file for six years (some provinces could keep it as long as seven years and Prince Edward Island keeps bankruptcies on file for 14 years). Information like failing to pay a credit card bill for several months will come off at the end of the six years in a systematic purge. That's why if you have had bad credit in the past there is hope to get your score back in shape.

How to Get Your Credit Score

By going to www.equifax.ca or www.transunion.ca and paying about $25, you can obtain both your credit score and credit report. If you have never checked your credit score, I would recommend that you do. You should check your credit history to make sure everything is correct. There is no need to check your credit score often but if your score is low, you may wish to check it again in a year or two to see if it has improved. It also doesn't hurt to check it before you apply for a loan so you will not have any surprises when you are sitting across from the bank manager. If you have a low credit score, you can work to improve it. You should check for mistakes and correct errors by contacting one of the credit reporting agencies. However, if the negative information is correct, it will remain on your credit file. You should close accounts you no longer use or need. (Just because you cut up a credit card, you still need to close down the account.) The most important thing you can do is pay your bills on time. This cannot be stressed enough. Also, don't let anyone make an inquiry about your credit score unless they absolutely have to, as repeated inquiries can lower your score.

To get your credit report free of charge, you can call Equifax at 1-800-465-7166 or write them at Equifax Canada Inc., Consumer Relations Department, Box 190 Jean Talon Station, Montreal, Quebec, H1S 2Z2. You can also call TransUnion at 1-800-663-9980 or write them at 170 Jackson Street East, Hamilton, Ontario, L8N 3K8. It will take 10 to 15 days before you get your credit report in the mail. When sending in for your credit file, you should include your name, including any maiden name, daytime and evening phone numbers, your current address and previous address (if you've moved in the past few years), your date of birth and marital status. Include your social insurance number and photocopies of two pieces of identification, such as a driver's licence or credit card. TransUnion also requires a photocopy of a utility bill. If you are requesting credit information for your spouse, then include their name, social insurance number and identification as well. Best of all, remember, this magic number has a huge impact on your life so always treat your credit rating and your credit score like gold as it really is that important. As for Bob Seger's tune, *Feel Like a Number*, if you are going to be assigned a number, you might as well make it a good one that will help you get ahead in life and not drag you down.

[25]
PROTECTING
YOUR IDENTITY

Identity theft and identity fraud is a huge problem. Scammers would love to pretend they are you to use your good reputation to open bank accounts, shop online or rent a car. Credit card companies are now more vigilant trying to stop identity theft not only because it's a hassle for you, but because it costs them tens of millions of dollars a year in losses. In fact, when I was on a family holiday in Old Orchard Beach, Maine this summer, my credit card was declined because my credit card company thought it was "suspicious" that I was in Maine. Wow, can't a person even take a holiday! I had this happen once before and usually call ahead to let the credit card company know that I will be out of the country. This time I didn't and they shut down the card in a hurry. It's just one phone call to get it reinstated, but it's still something you may want to consider if you plan to do some traveling. Call ahead and let them know where you are going so you don't get turned down if you're in the Stonehenge gift shop.

As I already talked about earlier, one of the most important things you have is your credit reputation. The last thing you need is some thief to mess up your credit rating and credit score, so you need to protect your private information carefully online, on the phone and in the mail. I have had CTV viewers tell me the nightmares they've had trying to get back their good name after scammers used their information to fraudulently obtain credit, cash cheques and open credit card accounts. Even when you have done nothing wrong, it could still have a negative impact on your financial situation. There are steps you can take to protect yourself against identity theft and if your personal information is compromised, there are ways to repair the damage and prevent future problems.

So how can someone steal your reputation? They may obtain your social insurance number, credit card numbers, driver's licence, passport or birth certificate. Thieves can steal credit and debit numbers through a process called "skimming" at tampered bank and point of sale machines, so if you are about to use a bank machine and something doesn't seem quite right—don't use it. Make sure your mail is safely stored and that bills are shredded before they are thrown in the garbage or recycling. Some scammers actually "dumpster dive"—a process where they search through trash to find credit card bills and banking information. Those personalized credit card offers you get in the mail need to be shredded before they go to the curb as they are one of the easiest ways a thief can get a credit card in your name. Crooks are getting so bold, they are also just phoning people up and asking them for their private and personal information. They may pose as someone from the bank, Microsoft or the government who wants to check your social insurance number, health card and other information. Unfortunately, it's not always strangers who steal information. Many people have had their identities stolen by people they knew or family members.

You should always pay close attention to your bank accounts, credit card statements and utility bills. If you see money missing from your accounts or charges you don't understand on your credit card bill, deal with them immediately. Credit card companies will almost always cover charges caused by identity theft but you must show that you informed them of the problem as soon as you noticed it. For example, if you lose your cell phone and call your cell phone provider right away, they can shut down your account. However, if you wait two weeks before calling them, then they could make you pay for all those long distance chats the thief made to Brazil. Never do banking or enter credit card numbers when using a Wi-Fi internet connection in a coffee shop, airport or hotel lobby. Thieves are able to monitor Wi-Fi internet connections to steal information. Banking online in your home or using a secure connection is safe, but check for a padlock or key icon at the bottom right of your browser to make sure the connection is safe and the information being sent is encrypted. Never respond to emails from banks, Revenue Canada or credit card companies that request personal information because they don't operate that way. These are just "phishing scams", hoping you'll simply hand over all your personal data. It's always wise to have up to date virus protection, not just to protect your computer but also your information, especially if you have your system connected to the internet 24 hours a day. Virus protection is updated constantly with most programs and now there are free programs that offer very good protection. These two get good reviews and are free.

- free.avg.com/us-en/free-antivirus-download
- www.avast.com/free-antivirus-download

If you do have your identity stolen you could end up having problems obtaining credit in the future as well as renting an apartment, getting a job or buying a car. To protect yourself, never carry your pin numbers in your wallet with your credit and debit cards. You should only carry your passport, social insurance number and birth certificate with you when you know you will need it. It's a good idea to also photocopy everything in your wallet and keep the photocopies in a safe place at home. It only takes a few minutes to lay all your cards out on a scanner or photocopier, and if you ever do have the unfortunate occasion to have your wallet lost or stolen, you will have copies of all your important cards and documents and will know who to contact quickly.

In some cases, a scammer may create phoney accounts in your name and use a different mailing address so you may not know there is a problem until you are turned down for credit. That's why it's a good idea to check your credit report every year or two to make sure everything is in order. If you lose credit cards, bank cards or any other important documents or information, call the corresponding companies right away. Generally, you will not be held responsible for any fraudulent activity. Call the police as well as Canada's major credit reporting agencies, TransUnion and Equifax. They will set up fraud alerts and monitor your accounts for any unusual activity. Having your identity stolen or tampered with is a major headache, but if you deal with it quickly, you can limit the damage to your credit reputation and keep your credit score in good standing.

[26]
PAYDAY LOAN SERVICES — A BAD IDEA

Stuck for cash? Need money in a hurry? A payday loan service would be happy to help you out—for a steep price. By definition a payday loan, also known as a paycheque advance, is a small, short-term loan intended to cover a borrower's expenses until his or her next payday. Sounds harmless enough, but the problem is the cost to borrow is high and once people start using this form of credit, they can easily get caught in an endless cycle of short term high interest loans.

Improvements have been made in the payday loan industry because when I first started doing stories on payday lending services a decade ago, these loans were almost the same as loan sharking. A loan shark is someone that offers unsecured loans at high interest rates to people often enforcing repayment by blackmail or threats of violence. No one was getting their legs broken, but I do remember interviewing a man who was in tears because he owed money to 13 different payday loan companies and he was constantly having to borrow from one lender to pay another. He was caught in a debt spiral of borrowing with no way out. The situation was so bad he rented out a room to a stranger in his rented Toronto apartment to try and get ahead.

Payday loan services in Canada are a billion dollar business that continues to grow. There are about 1,500 pay day services across the country with about half of them in Ontario. Loans are usually for about 50 per cent of the borrower's net pay. The average loan is approximately $300 with a term of 10 days to two weeks. There are now restrictions on how much interest, administrative costs and added fees a payday lender can charge. It was the Association of Community·Organizations for

93

Reform Now, known as ACORN that was first to sound alarm bells on the high fees and interest rates payday lenders were charging. ACORN argued that interest rates charged by payday lenders should be criminal under Canadian law. According to section 347 of the Criminal Code, annual interest rates for loans must not exceed 60%. ACORN calculated if someone were to borrow $400 for two weeks, with a lending fee charged of $51.84 that was an annual interest rate of 1,092%.

The Payday Loan Industry says it's unfair to assign annual interest rates to short term loans and has argued that it provides a necessary service to help Canadians who have trouble meeting the financial obligations before their next payday. The industry claims payday lending allows Canadians to get small, short-term loans without having to ask friends or family for help. After concerns were raised, provinces started to crack down on the high fees charged by payday lenders. In Ontario, the government ruled that a payday lender can charge no more than $21 for every $100 that a consumer borrows. Rollover loans (where someone takes one payday loan to help pay off another) are not allowed. There is also a two day cooling off period if you change your mind and you are allowed to cancel the contract with no questions asked and no penalty.

Bottom line? You want to be careful to never be in such a financial crunch where you feel the need to go to a payday lender. You may think a quick loan will help you get over a financial hump, but it will just drive you further into debt. If you or someone you know is using a payday loan company, than there are probably other, more deeply rooted, financial problems that should be dealt with. Make up your mind that you will never darken a payday lender's door.

[27]
DECLARING BANKRUPTCY—
DON'T DO IT

By definition, bankruptcy is the legal process that declares a person or business to be insolvent and absolves that person's or business' debts. Put simply, it's when you run out of money and can't pay your bills. When I was young I had a friend who was a big spender. He was always buying expensive clothes, dining out and generally blowing every cent he had. As he got older this pattern of spending continued and he bought himself a luxury sports car to keep up with his high profile appearance and high spending ways. In his twenties he had dug himself into debt so deep he couldn't keep up with his car payments, credit card bills and his rent so he said "no big deal—I'll just declare bankruptcy." He did and it caused him financial problems for many years. Not everyone who declares bankruptcy is a reckless spender or someone on unemployment or welfare racking up bills with no intention of paying them back. In fact, most are working steadily with a reasonable income. Many consumers who turn to bankruptcy are middle class people in their 30s and 40s who are going through a life changing event such as a sickness, divorce or losing their job.

A 2010 study by Bankruptcy Trustees Hoyes, Michalos & Associates Inc. found that the average bankrupt person looks a lot like the average Canadian. Douglas Hoyes says, "We recently examined approximately 8,000 personal insolvencies filed in 2009 and 2010 and we discovered that a typical insolvent person, who we call "Joe Debtor", is a male, 41 years old. He has one dependent and has a monthly income of around $2,240, close to the Canadian average of just over $2,400. He is not that different than the average Canadian." According to the study, the major problem is that Joe Debtor is a big spender with a lot of debt. The average Canadian has consumer credit, excluding mortgages, of $16,399. Joe Debtor owes almost $60,000. Joe Debtor is also loaded down with credit card debt of almost $24,400. More than half of those who declared bankruptcy owed money on four or more credit cards.

The study also found that most Canadians in financial difficulty are decent, hardworking people, but due to divorce, job loss, a health crisis and over-use of credit, they are forced into bankruptcy. The study found that 39% of those declaring bankruptcy said job loss or reduced incomes contributed to their financial problems. Fourteen percent blamed a relationship break-up while 55% admitted that they were over-extended and mismanaged their finances. Despite good health care in Canada, 12% listed health reasons (injury, disability, medical conditions) as a cause of their insolvency.

TYPICAL BANKRUPTCY CLIENT

Joe Debtor

Personal Information

Gender	Male
Average age	41
Marital status	Married
Average family size	2 (including debtor)
Average monthly income	$2,240 net of deductions
Average month income for all Canadians	$2,419(1)
Total unsecured debt	$59,814
Likelihood they own a home	26% (1 in 4 debtors)
Average mortgage value	$210,574

Joe Debtors Debts Include

Bank loans	$13,761
Credit cards	$24,390
Taxes	$5,412
Finance company loans	$4,997
Student loans	$1,945
Other	$9,309

The events that lead to bankruptcy are quite predictable and bankruptcy trustees see the same signs over and over again. Even if you have a good job, a home, a car and everything seems fine, a life changing event can put many people into serious financial problems in just two weeks because so many people are living from one paycheque to the next. It's why being wise with your money is so important early in your life. Not overspending, having bad habits or expensive tastes can help you avoid being in a position where you may have to declare bankruptcy. Declaring bankruptcy is not a decision to be made lightly and as host of CTV's *Consumer Report*, I often hear from people who regret having done it. It will affect your credit history for seven full years and be permanently kept on file in Ottawa in a national database. At any time someone can check to see if you have ever declared bankruptcy—not a great legacy to leave behind.

If you are having financial problems, you should seek credit counselling for advice. You may also be eligible for a Consumer Proposal which is a legal procedure for consumers who are experiencing financial difficulties, but can still afford to repay a portion of their debts. You might be able to work out a payment plan with your creditors and if it's accepted, it becomes a legally binding settlement of your unsecured debts. If you owed $50,000 you may be able to work out a payment plan over four years to pay back a portion, but not all of the debt. You could seek an extension of time for payment, reductions in interest rates and repayment of less than 100 cents on the dollar.

If bankruptcy is the only way out, everything you own will be turned over to the trustee, who will notify all creditors of your bankruptcy and ensure that they will no longer seek payment outside of the bankruptcy process. You will be required to attend financial counselling and be in bankruptcy for a minimum of nine months, and during that time you will have to submit monthly statements of your income and expenses. You will lose any equity in your home and car, although your RRSP will not be affected except for contributions made in the year before you went bankrupt. Student loans are also wiped out if you have not been a student for more than seven years and in cases of "hardship", you may apply to bankruptcy court after five years to have a student loan reduced or discharged. However, according to Douglas Hoyes, "even if your student loan was more than seven years old when you went bankrupt, the government could object, and you could still end up being required to pay some or all of it back." So don't think a bankruptcy is an automatic way to avoid paying off a student loan. Once a bankruptcy is under way, the trustee will sell your assets and use the money to pay off as much debt as possible. Any remaining debt, except for court fines, alimonies or child support is then legally eliminated. You can keep your clothing, furniture and tools if they are required for your job.

If you declare bankruptcy, banks and other lenders will see you as a bad risk and you will have a difficult time getting a loan, credit card or other financing. You may have to apply for a secured credit card, which means you have to pay the bank up front to hold funds for you, so if you use your credit card, you could actually end up paying interest on your own money! You will have to tell potential lenders you have declared bankruptcy even though they will know anyway, and if you do get credit, you will have to pay extremely high interest rates because you are a credit risk. To add insult to financial injury, you will have to pay about $1,500 to declare personal bankruptcy! As I mentioned, the information will roll off your credit rating in seven years, unless you have been bankrupt more than once, but it's permanently listed in Ottawa for anyone to check for the rest of your life and beyond. Make the right financial decisions so bankruptcy is an option you'll never have to consider.

PART FOUR

[28]
SAVING MONEY—
INVESTING FOR THE FUTURE

"I'm involved in the stock market, which is fun and sometimes, very painful."

Regis Philbin
Television talk show host

This book is all about saving money and then investing your savings so your hard earned dollars will grow over a lifetime. You can invest in yourself, in real estate or in a business, but for the vast majority of us who are busy with our lives, families and jobs, the stock market is often the easiest place to put our money with hopes that it will double, triple and quadruple. Having said that, investing is not always easy to do and it comes with its own risks, rewards, stresses and successes. Of course, you don't have to be in the stock market and there are many people who have gone through their lives without ever buying a single stock or share in a company. However, for many people the stock market is a good place to have at least have a portion of your savings and I'll tell you why in a moment.

First of all, you should know there are no guarantees in the stock market that the shares you buy will increase in price. Even if you buy stock in a good company there can be outside factors which could impact your investments. There are bull markets where stock prices will rise quickly, and bear markets where they will fall rapidly. It can be a stressful roller coaster ride. Then there are major corrections that can lead to recessions. During the Roaring Twenties it was the golden age for radio, TV, car manufacturing, the telephone and aviation. These were boom times and companies saw their stocks soar, but on Black Tuesday the stock market came crashing down. It was the Great Wall Street Crash of 1929 which gave way to the Great Depression of the 1930s.

In the fall of 2008, this generation suffered its own stock market meltdown with Black October. That's when the Toronto Stock Exchange dropped from its high of over 15,000 points to a low of 8,000, losing almost half its value in a month. These were scary times for investors and I can tell you that first hand. Watching your investments plummet like a stone not knowing whether you should sell or hold on was a stomach churning feeling. When it happens it makes you wonder why you are in the stock market at all. So why be in the stock market?

I put this question to Larry Berman, the Co-Founder of ETF Capital Management, and the host of the popular Business News Network Show (BNN) *Berman's Call*. Berman has twenty years of industry experience and is ranked as one of Canada's top technical analysts. On his program, Berman provides a technical and fundamental analysis to try and give investors an edge in the stock market. Anyone who has been in the stock market long enough has their share of stock stories that went wrong. Berman says when you are young, there is a temptation to take risk because there can be great rewards when you are right. However, the results can be financially devastating when you are wrong. Berman says, "If you have $10,000 starting out in a portfolio and you invest it in a junior company that may or may not fly, sure it could be worth $100,000 in a year, but it could also be worth zero. You always have to ask yourself how much risk do you want to take."

Berman says he is now a very conservative investor because of something that happened to him early in his life. He says "I learned this lesson when I was in my mid-twenties and my wife and I were just getting married. We were putting money away and I worked in the industry and one of the analysts at the firm that I worked with loved this copper company. He said it was going to have the biggest find in the world and everyone in the firm got into it, including me. I felt it was such a sure thing I bought stock on margin (borrowing money to buy stock) and I even used my credit cards because it was a supposed to be such a sure thing. When a negative report came out on Monday, the stock dropped from $20 to $12. I was wiped out because I was leveraged. My wife didn't understand that, and I looked at her and I said that's tuition that I paid to learn a lesson and it's a lesson that I'm never going to repeat again."

Berman is now one of Canada's most successful market analysts and admittedly almost everyone who invests in the stock market at one time or another has paid "tuition" to learn a lesson about investing. However, if you are careful you may not have to. Berman says, "The amount of risk you're willing to take when you're investing is an important factor and it's going to be different for everyone. If someone is 20 years old and they are lucky enough to inherit some money and they have a substantial portfolio, they can afford more risk than someone who doesn't.

I was in a position when I started with no money and only debt and it was a stupid thing to do. That's probably why I'm generally conservative now and manage money for people."

Andrew Cook is a portfolio manager with Andrew Cook and Associates, and is a successful money manager who co-managed one of Canada's most successful resource funds. He currently manages a resource mutual fund worth tens of millions of dollars and has keen insight into the ups and downs of the stock market. I asked him, if there is so much volatility, why should young Canadians put their hard earned dollars at risk? Cook says there are a number of reasons why young people should have exposure to the stock market. Cook says, "The first is economic. Over the long term equities have demonstrated a greater return than bonds or cash. Starting early gives individuals a longer period of time to benefit from the powerful impact of compounding, in an asset class with strong long term returns. Simply put, a person needs to invest less money when they are young in order to generate a given amount, than when they are older."

Cook says that investing in the stock market early also starts the learning process earlier. If you make a mistake when you are young, this is not as traumatic as if you make a mistake when you are older and have more money to lose. He says, "People also begin to understand their own risk tolerance much earlier, a point which I think is extremely important as they get older and have more money. By understanding their personal risk tolerance and with greater education, hopefully they won't panic when markets fall or get euphoric when they rise and make moves that could be detrimental to their financial well-being." Cook also says that investing in the stock market is a form of forced savings. "Money that is invested is money that otherwise could be spent. This helps develop spending discipline which is extremely important to build financial security." Another reason to invest is that even with all the ups and downs of the stock market, over the past 40 years money invested in the stock market has generally been able to realize returns of 6% to 8%, even in balanced or relatively conservative investments. Money stuck in a savings account or under your mattress won't do that, and as you can see from the interest rate tables in the chapter on the power of compound interest, every point higher you can get will make a huge difference over 10 to 50 years. This is why you should have at least some of your money in the stock market, but how much, and how much risk you want to take is up to you.

[29]
PAYING YOURSELF FIRST

If you can master this one simple aspect of personal finance, it can start you off on the right track and help you to build wealth over a lifetime. It is a very simple idea—pay yourself first. That's it. Many of us aren't very good at budgeting, but we are very good at spending, so just decide to spend money on yourself every time you get paid and make it automatic. This concept is now accepted as the most basic of common sense financial planning. The idea of paying yourself first was popularized more than 20 years ago by David Chilton who wrote *The Wealthy Barber*, the best-selling book in Canadian publishing. David Bach, author of *The Automatic Millionaire*, continued the pay yourself first idea by advising that you should "automatically" have money taken off your paycheque and then invested before you have a chance to spend it. A very simple idea, but a powerful message and here is why.

Most of us are very good at paying our bills. We don't miss payments to the cell phone, cable or gas company. We pay the rent or our mortgage on time. The problem is that if we get paid $1,000 on payday, it's human nature to want to spend whatever is left after we pay our bills. If we have to pay out $688 in bills then yippee! That means there is $312 to blow! So why not go to the club, a restaurant or a concert? The bills are paid, what could be the problem? That's where the concept of paying yourself first comes in. Make the payment to yourself be every bit as important as one to the electric company. You simply add one more payment to your bills every two weeks. You can set up an automatic payroll deduction plan where $100 comes off your paycheque and goes into a savings or investment account before you ever see it (both an RRSP or TFSA are great options which I will talk about later in this

103

book). Paying yourself first is also known as "forced savings", and even if the person who had $312 left over, put away that $100 into a forced savings plan, they would still have $212 left to spend.

Once you start a pay yourself plan, eventually you won't miss the money coming off your paycheque and as you pay down debt or get a raise you should try to increase the amount to $150 to $200 a paycheque. Ten percent of your salary is considered the magic number to invest which can be hard to do, but imagine how much that could add up to over a lifetime of saving.

There is only one drawback to the forced savings plan and that is lack of discipline on the spending side. It's fantastic if you are saving $400 a month in a forced savings plan, but if you are running up credit card debt and other bills of $400 on the spending side, this will offset any gains you're are making. As Chilton says, "You have to live within your means. That is 90% of the financial planning game." So keep in mind as you pay yourself first, this does not mean you can pile on debt on the other side of the ledger, especially high interest debt. If you can embrace this concept of "paying yourself first", "saving automatically" or "forced savings" whatever you want to call it—then you will be on the road to saving and you will be amazed how quickly the money adds up.

[30]
THE POWER OF
COMPOUND INTEREST

Albert Einstein gave us the *Theory of Relativity* and is regarded as the father of modern physics. He is said to have made the following quote about compound interest, but there is some debate over whether or not he coined the phrase "The most powerful force in the universe is compound interest."

Some argue that compound interest is such a powerful formula, that it is simply attributed to one of the smartest men who ever lived. Think of compound interest like a snowball at the top of a hill. It's small at first, but as it rolls down the hill gathering momentum and snow, it gets larger and larger and by the time it reaches the bottom, it's a massive size. It's the same with starting an investment savings account early in life. It's small at first, but as years go by it gathers momentum and the sooner you begin to save, the less saving you actually have to do. That may sound hard to believe, but it's the power of compound interest at work. When you're young, you have many other bills to worry about, but if you can "pay yourself first", meaning if you can always manage to put money into an investment account every month or every year, you begin the process of making compound interest work for you.

Here are a few examples of the power of compound interest. Imagine that you put $100 a month into an investment account every month for 60 years. I know that's a long time, but $100 a month is only $25 a week which someone could certainly do without too much difficulty.

SAVING $100 A MONTH

Years of Saving	Amount Invested	Invested at 6%	Invested at 10%
10	$12,000	$16,765	$21,037
20	$24,000	$46,791	$75,603
30	$36,000	$100,562	$217,132
40	$48,000	$196,857	$584,222
50	$60,000	$396,307	$1,536,359
60	$72,000	$678,139	$4,005,957

As you can see, the $100 a month turns into $678,139 with an annual rate of return of 6% and into over $4,000,000 at 10% interest over 60 years. You can also see that to get that 4 million dollars, you need to invest only $72,000 of your own money—the rest is the power of compound interest. Let's look at another example, because chances are you are going to want to get at your money before 60 years. If we were to invest $200 a month over 40 years let's see what we would end up with. If you begin saving at 22 years old and you would have a large amount by the time you turn 62.

SAVING $200 A MONTH

Years of Saving	Amount Invested	Invested at 6%	Invested at 10%
10	$24,000	$33,531	$42,074
20	$48,000	$93,582	$151,206
30	$72,000	$201,124	$434,264
40	$96,000	$393,714	$1,168,444

If you were able to get a return of 10% on your money you would have over a million dollars in 40 years from investing just $50 a week. Of course, the goal is to save even more than this, but you can see if you just stayed with one amount, due to the magic of compound interest you would still end up with a fairly substantial sum. Here is just one more example to show you the benefit of starting early. Let's say Connor and his sister Bridget decided to save $2,000 a year in their investment account. Connor starts saving immediately and puts $2,000 a year into his account. Bridget decides to wait until she is 28 years old to start saving. However, when Connor turns 28 years old he gets married, buys a house and no longer makes payments into his investment account. He does however leave the money in his account, and again, this is where you can see the power of compound interest at work. We will use an annual interest rate of 10% for this example.

Age	Connor	Bridget
22	$2,200	0
23	$4,620	0
24	$7,282	0
25	$10,210	0
26	$13,431	0
27	$16,979	0
28	$20,871	$2,200
29	$22,958	$4,620
30	$25,253	$7,282
35	$40,670	$20,871
40	$60,499	$47,045
45	$105,488	$89,198
50	$169,889	$157,086
55	$273,608	$266,419
60	$440,449	$442,503
65	$709,670	$726,086

So as you can see even though Connor invested only $12,000, because he did it early and left it alone, his investment grew to almost the same amount as Bridget's and don't forget, Bridget had to contribute $2,000 a year, every year from the age of 28, until she turned 65 which is $74,000. With the power of compound interest, the earlier you start saving, the greater the accumulated interest on your original investment will be. Just look at the difference those first six years meant for Connor. As the old saying goes the best time to plant a tree would have been 20 years ago, but the second best time is today. So if you have not started an investment savings account get one started now, even if you can only contribute $25 a month. Work to increase it when you can afford to.

To take advantage of the power of compound interest:
- Start as early as possible
- Create a savings program and stick to it
- Don't touch the money as compounding only works if you allow your investment to grow

Now that you know about the power of compound interest, you want to make sure you put your money where it can grow tax free. You can do this by placing your money in a Registered Retirement Savings Plan or a Tax Free Savings Account, which we will talk about in the chapters ahead.

[31]
THE POWER OF
DOLLAR COST AVERAGING

Dollar cost averaging is a strategy where you buy a fixed dollar amount of an investment on a regular basis regardless of what the share price is. This is a great strategy for long term investing and it can take the guess work out of buying stocks or mutual funds. The idea being, that if you put the same amount of money into an investment every month you will get more shares when prices are low, and fewer shares when prices are higher. Over time the cost of the shares will average out. This strategy also helps you spread the risk, because it prevents you from buying a large amount of stock all at once which could be a mistake if the market drops substantially.

Let's take a look at dollar cost averaging in action. We will say that Amanda is going to buy $400 worth of a single mutual fund every month for 12 months. Since she is spending the same amount of money every month, when the share price drops she is able to buy more shares.

DOLLAR COST AVERAGING TABLE

Month	Amount	Price	Shares
1	$400	$8	50
2	$400	$10	40
3	$400	$ 7	57.1
4	$400	$5	80
5	$400	$7	57.1
6	$400	$6	66.7
7	$400	$9	44.4
8	$400	$7	57.1
9	$400	$8	50
10	$400	$6	66.7
11	$400	$8	50
12	$400	$9	44.4

After One Year	Total Invested	Average Share Price	Total Number of Shares
	$4,800	$7.50	720.6

If at year end the share price was at 9 dollars you would then have 720.6 shares x $9 share price = $6,485.40

That's a profit of $1,685.40. You have less risk and when the price drops you don't need to be as concerned, because you are simply buying more shares at the reduced price which is the beauty of dollar cost averaging. Most people that use the dollar cost averaging strategy do so by purchasing mutual funds on a monthly basis. It works well with mutual funds because once your initial investment is made, you don't have to pay a commission on each transaction. Instead with mutual funds you will pay a Management Expense Ratio or MER, something we will talk about more in the next chapter.

Dollar cost averaging is part of a long term strategy that also includes the power of compounding and investing in a tax sheltered investment vehicle such as a Registered Retirement Savings Plan (RRSP) and a Tax Free Savings Account (TFSA). Stock markets are constantly in a state of flux going up one day and down the next. Using a dollar cost averaging strategy will allow you to take advantage of when the market is down; taking the guesswork and temptation out of trying to time the market. Of course, it will be the final share price that will determine how much your investment is worth, however; if you buy good quality investments and use dollar cost averaging over a long period of time, you will have better luck than guessing when the best time is to buy stocks or mutual funds. Best of all, when the market does take a dip, you can feel good knowing that you are continuing to buy your investments on sale.

[32]
STOCKS, MUTUAL FUNDS
AND EXCHANGE TRADED FUNDS

When it comes to investing you have many different options. Some are conservative and some are risky. Here is a breakdown of some of the places where you can put your money.

- **Cash:** This is just leaving your money in cash and accepting whatever interest rate the bank will give you. This is extremely safe, but the amount of money you make is minimal. If you put $10,000 in the bank and the interest rate you were receiving was 2%, after one year you would have $10,200. Not much of a return.
- **Bonds:** Bonds are issued by governments, companies, banks and public utilities. If you were to buy a bond of $10,000, you are given a set rate of interest for a set period of time. At the end of the term you get your money back plus interest. If a bond had an interest rate of 3% you would get $10,300 back. Again a very safe investment with a limited return.
- **GICs:** A GIC is a Guaranteed Income Certificate and it's similar to a bond. Most GICs pay you a set rate of interest for a set length of time. Some GICs base what you get on the performance of a benchmark, such as a stock exchange index. If you were able to secure a 4% interest rate, your $10,000 would be $10,400 at year end.
- **Stocks:** Here is where it gets interesting. When you own a stock you own a share in a company. You could own "blue chip stocks" which are shares in well-established and financially sound companies. Blue chips generally sell high-quality, widely accepted products and services. The name "blue

chip" comes from the game of poker because blue chips have the highest value. Blue chip stocks often pay dividends, so you are also given a share of the company's profits on a periodic basis. You could also buy penny stocks that trade at a relatively low price and are generally considered to be highly speculative and high risk. If you put your $10,000 in a blue-chip bank stock, and the bank had a good year, you could have gains of 10%. You would then have $11,000 at year end. However, if you put your $10,000 in a penny stock mining company and it had a bad year, you could be down 50% and your $10,000 could be worth $5,000. However, if the mining company found gold, your stock could triple to $30,000.

- **Mutual Funds:** A Mutual Fund is a collection of different stocks. It may also be a combination of stocks and bonds. They are generally much safer than picking individual stocks because you are buying into a fund with many other shareholders. For example, a mutual fund could own 100 different companies. This spreads the risk because if one company has a bad year and its stock goes down, another one may have a good year. Mutual funds are generally less volatile. You also can buy into certain market sectors such as precious metals, consumer goods and financial companies. The upside is the fund is professionally managed. The downside is that you have to pay the manager a fee known as an MER, or Management Expensive Ratio. The fees are generally in the area of 2.5%, so if you had $10,000 invested every year, you have to pay the mutual fund company $250 as a management fee, whether the fund makes money or not. Mutual funds can also have sale commissions which will lessen your returns. Generally investors will own several different funds with varying degrees of risk. They are also attractive because they are a convenient way to invest as you can set up a monthly investment program, and have funds automatically transferred from your bank account.

- **Exchange Traded Funds (ETFs):** An ETF is a security that tracks an index, a commodity or a basket of assets like an index fund, but trades like a stock on an exchange. Whatever the index is doing, you will match it. So you won't be higher than the market, but you won't be lower either. You will be average and that can be a good thing. An investor can do anything with an ETF that they can do with a normal stock and because ETFs are traded on stock exchanges, they can be bought and sold at any time during the day. ETFs are growing in popularity because of their low fees. While the average MER for mutual funds is between 2.25 % and 2.5 %, MERs for ETF fees start as low as 0.15 % with many available for 0.5% to 0.75%.

- **Index Mutual Funds:** This is a fund that is really a cross between a mutual fund and an ETF. It's a type of mutual fund with a portfolio constructed to match or track the components of a market index. They provide broad market exposure, low operating expenses and low portfolio turnover. While you have to pay a commission every time you buy an ETF, you don't have to with an index fund so it's easy to set up a monthly investment program. Every Canadian bank offers them and the MERs are in the range of 0.85% to 1.5%, about half the MER of a regular mutual fund.

Since ETFs are currently gaining in popularity with Canadian investors, due to their ease of use and low fees, I asked Larry Berman, co-founder of ETF Capital Management, why they may be a good fit for young investors. Berman says, "Canada was the first market in the world to have exchange traded market funds. An ETF is simply a fund that is representing an index and that index could be pretty much anything. It could be a bond index, it could be a stock index, it could be an index of shipping companies; you name it, if there an index you can create a fund on it. The media portrays ETFs as a cheaper alternative to mutual funds, which they absolutely are. If your advisor is going to do nothing for you other than rebalance your portfolio once a year and you're just kind of holding the market, then you might as well use ETFs."

You do need to be knowledgeable about asset allocation, risk and how to construct a portfolio, but he says investors who are tired of paying high fees for mutual funds when they are seeing little growth may want to switch to ETFs. "With ETFs you're going to have a lower annual management fee and all things being equal, you're going to do better on the compounding effect of having that lower management cost. You're still subject to the exact same market risks that you would in any mutual fund that tries to track or beat any given index." Berman says it makes sense to cross over to ETFs instead of being with a mutual fund company. "When you're in your early twenties finishing school you probably have debt, but it's really the best time to get your money in the market and use dollar cost averaging to compound for long periods of time." I also had to ask one of Canada's top analysts just what the stock market will do over the next three to five years. Berman says, "The markets will go up, down, up, down, up, down, up, down. Young people need to educate themselves and I think you've got to trade as there will be lots of opportunities and opportunity comes in understanding and education as opposed to being passive about it and just saying whatever it is, it is." To not put all your eggs in one basket you can also hold several kinds of investments. Some bonds, some mutual funds, some ETFs and an index fund. This can be a good way to start out as you learn about investments and learn about your own tolerance for risk.

[33]
THE TAX FREE SAVINGS ACCOUNT

You may not realize it yet, but the Tax Free Savings Account is the best investment vehicle to happen in your lifetime—mine too! Normally when you put money in the bank, invest in the stock market or other kinds of investments, the government wants a cut of your profit. For example, if you put $5,000 in a stock and it doubled to $10,000, the taxman wants a percentage of the profits. So of that $5,000 you made, you may have to give Ottawa up to $2,000, depending on your tax bracket. With the Tax Free Savings Account (TFSA) you can save up to $5,000 annually and it will grow tax free, plus you can take the money out at any time without paying a penalty. The TFSA is different from the Registered Retirement Savings Plan or RRSP which we will talk about in the next chapter.

It was on January 1, 2009, the Canadian government decided every Canadian can save $5,000 annually in a TFSA. For couples that's $10,000 in tax free savings. Canada's Finance Minister Jim Flaherty, who created the TFSA, called it the most important investment vehicle for Canadians to be introduced since the creation of the RRSP in 1957. Flaherty told me, "We already have a retirement plan. This is a savings plan for everything else."

The TFSA is similar to a RRSP, in that everything you put into the plan is allowed to grow tax free. The difference is that you do not receive a tax deduction the same way you do when you put money in an RRSP. However, this is where it gets interesting because everything in a TFSA grows completely tax free and you can withdraw it at any time without paying a tax penalty! So if you have put in $10,000 and it has grown to $14,000 you can take out the entire $14,000 without paying any tax on it.

This means you could use a TFSA to save for a down payment on a home, a car, or a wedding and when you take money out not one cent will go to the government.

RRSPs have always been an important savings vehicle, but I have never liked the way you can't take out your own money without paying a huge tax penalty (more on that in the next chapter). It's why you should try to open a TFSA as soon as possible if you haven't already. Inside a TFSA you can hold cash, stocks, bonds, or any other investment you like. You have to be at least 18 years old to open a TFSA account and for parents who may want to help their children get a start in life, this is an excellent place to gift money so it can grow tax free.

If a couple were each to contribute $5,000 to a TFSA for five years and, assuming an annual return of eight percent, they would have about $63,400 in five years. Of course, setting aside $5,000 a year for a TFSA is not easy, but with automatic payment plans you can set up a TFSA and have money automatically come off your paycheque. Start with $50 a month; move up to $100 when you are able and $200 after that. The magic of compound interest, dollar cost averaging and tax free savings make this the ideal place to save for your future.

How much money you save depends on your income level and marginal tax rate as to how much money the tax free savings plan will save you over time. The higher your income, the higher your savings will be. For this example, I used someone with an income between $40,000 and $80,000:

EXAMPLE 1	EXAMPLE 2
Tax Free Savings Account	**Tax Free Savings Account**
Save $5,000 annually	Save $5,000 annually
For 10 years	For 25 years
9% growth	9% growth
Tax Free Savings Account	**Tax Free Savings Account**
Tax free savings account $79,309	Tax free savings account $442,152
In taxable account $71,823	In taxable account $331,910
Tax savings $7,486	Tax savings $110,242

Those tax savings are huge and a nine percent return is possible. Even balanced funds offered through most major banks have been able to return eight percent annually over 40 years. Also, the higher the income the higher the tax saving will be. Once you open a TFSA the next decision is what are you going to put into it? I would argue that you don't want to be too aggressive with risky stocks or commodities, but nor do you want to be too passive with bonds and cash. In the chapter *The Power of Dollar Cost Averaging*, we looked at the benefits of monthly contributions into various mutual funds, annual or semi-annual purchases of shares in Exchange Traded Funds (ETFs) or buying blue chip stocks such as Canadian banks. I believe this is the best way to make use of dollar cost averaging and holding something inside your TFSA that actually has a chance to grow, allowing you to receive a tax free benefit. If you decide to invest in stocks or riskier investments inside a TFSA, you should also know that while losses can be deducted from your income in a regular non-registered trading account, they cannot be within a TFSA.

Once you learn about the benefits of a TFSA and a RRSP, you will have to decide which a better savings vehicle for you is. The correct answer is to do both. Max out your RRSP contributions and max out your $5,000 TFSA contributions. Easy to say— difficult to do. A great thing about the TFSA is that funds can be withdrawn at any time without penalty, so if you do need money for a new baby, a new car or a down payment on a cottage, you can take the money out without paying tax. Another plus is that unused contribution space can be carried forward and any withdrawals can be put back into the TFSA at a later date. Some experts do worry that because the money is so easy to get at, many Canadians will not use it as a long term savings vehicle.

This is also important to note. If you take out money from your TFSA, you have to wait until the next calendar year to put money back in. Many Canadians were caught off guard when they took money out of their TFSAs in March and then deposited the money back in July. They were shocked that the government considered that a double payment for the year and were charged a tax penalty of one percent a month tax on your over contribution. For some people that meant an unexpected tax bill of about $500. Once you open your TFSA, talk to your banker before making any withdrawals to make sure you fully understand the process.

If you are unsure how much contribution room you have left in your TFSA, you can call a government hotline to find out. Just call 1-800-267-6999, and press option #6. The General Information service gives you information on a number of topics concerning the Tax Free Savings Account and it's available 24 hours a day, seven days a week. The service lets you know the amount of unused TFSA contributions as of January 1st of the current year. To use the hotline you require the following:

- your social insurance number;
- your month and year of birth; and
- the total income you entered on line 150 of your return.

There is also an excellent Tax Free Savings Calculator at the following website: www.budget.gc.ca/2008/mm/calc_e.html

For more information on tax Free Savings Accounts:

www.cra-arc.gc.ca/tx/ndvdls/tpcs/tfsa-celi/menu-eng.html

If there is one thing you get out of this book, I would say it is this—open a Tax Free Savings Account with your bank, start contributing every month whatever you can into equity, balanced or bond mutual funds. The perfect amount to contribute would be $415 a month, which would bring you under the allowable $5,000 yearly amount. Once you get enough money into it, in a few years, you can then seek financial advice from an expert on what to do next.

[34]
RRSPs

Now that we've just read about Canada's newest tax saving vehicle, The Tax Free Savings Account, let's talk about the original tax savings plan that has been around for more than 50 years—the Registered Retirement Savings Plan, or RRSP. The government wants us to look after ourselves in our retirement and even if you are just starting out in life, Ottawa wants you to open and contribute to an RRSP. It is a good idea and here is why.

For every dollar you put into an RRSP, you get a tax break from the government upfront! And as your RRSP nest egg grows, it is sheltered from tax. One can view an RRSP like your own personal bank vault, where you put money in and it grows every year, shielded from taxes. The big plus when you contribute to an RRSP is, at tax time, the government wants to thank you for being so responsible that they send you a tax refund cheque in the spring! You can contribute up to 18% of your income to your RRSP and the more money you make, the bigger the tax break you get.

If you contribute $5,000 in one year and are in a 40% tax bracket, you will get an immediate tax savings of $2,000. If you are in a 54% tax bracket, you will save $2,700. That is money that the government gives back to you right away, so investing in an RRSP is a no-brainer right? Well, yes and no.

Here are some of the issues surrounding RRSPs that are important to consider. The government gives you a tax break in the form of a cheque at tax time and if you take that $2,700 tax refund and immediately put it into your RRSP for the next year, pay off a loan or even stick it in a Tax Free Savings Account, then yes, you will be getting ahead. But if you are like many Canadians, you will use that $2,700 to fund a trip to Barbados to get away from our cold Canadian winter. Also, the government gives you a tax break now, but when you take that money out in the future, they want the tax break back. Yup. That's why when you talk to a retired person, you may find they are not as enthusiastic about RRSPs because they know "RRSPs equal tax deferral—not necessarily tax savings." Another potential negative is if you ever decide that the $40,000 you have in your RRSP would be better off as a down payment on a cottage, your bank treats your RRSP funds as if they are not even there. It's like MC Hammer's rap song *U Can't Touch This!* Want to use your RRSP to pay down debt? *U Can't Touch This!* Want to use your RRSP for a home renovation? *U Can't Touch This!* If you are ever stuck and must take money out of your RRSP, you are taxed so heavily, depending on your tax bracket, you could lose up to half the money you are taking out, meaning, you guessed it—*U Can't Touch This!*

Now I should say I believe that everyone should have some money in an RRSP to take advantage of that big refund check the government will send you in the spring. But the best way to get ahead is to reinvest the tax refund, which unfortunately most of us don't. If you can, you will definitely be ahead of the game and make an RRSP work for you the way it's designed to. Since it's hard to come up with thousands of dollars all at once when the RRSP deadline comes around every spring, a good approach is to use the dollar cost averaging strategy, contributing every paycheque or every month even if it's just $50 or $100. You can also load up your RRSP with any investment vehicles you want such as GICs, savings bonds, mutual funds and stocks.

If you have a spouse, you may wish to contribute to an RRSP plan for the spouse who is the lower income earner. You will get the same tax break as if you'd invested in your own name now, but when the money is withdrawn in the future it will be taxed at a lower rate. If you don't have enough money to put into an RRSP, banks make it very easy to borrow so you can make a contribution. This can be a wise move if you use the refund cheque you receive at tax time to pay back the loan. If you don't, you've just taken on more debt. You can also catch up on missed RRSP contributions, but don't over contribute more than $2,000 or you will be penalized.

So as a young person, you may wonder when you can get your hands on that money you're putting into your RRSP every year. The idea is for you to take it out only when you retire, when your total income is reduced so you will pay less tax. Even if you don't want to take it out, as soon as you turn 71 years old, you must convert it into a RIFF (don't worry, you don't need to know about a RIFF for many years) and you are then forced to start withdrawing it. Why? Well because the government wants its tax money back and that's when it will collect it. Of course, by this time you will be retired and instead of making $85,000 a year, you may have a reduced income of $50,000 a year, so you'll pay less in tax. Another important factor is whether or not you are part of a company pension plan. If you are, RRSP contributions are not as crucial. But if you don't have a pension or you are self-employed, you should be taking full advantage of what an RRSP has to offer.

Bottom line—RRSP or TFSA? I personally like the Tax Free Saving Account and think if a person could actually start at 25 years old putting in $5,000 a year, every year until they retire, they really would have a nice nest egg for the future. Of course, the correct answer is do both which can be very difficult to do. I believe what is most important is to have a balanced portfolio, money invested in an RRSP, money invested in a TFSA, money invested in your home and savings. If you can do all of this, you will be on the right track to financial security.

[35]
DOING YOUR TAXES—
ADVICE FROM AN EXPERT

You may remember your parents complaining about taxes or if you are already part of the working world, you may be complaining yourself. Canada is the greatest country in the world to live in, but our system is such that we fund it through taxation and we pay a lot of tax. Federal taxes, provincial taxes, municipal property tax, income tax, health taxes, gas taxes, entertainment taxes, taxes on alcohol and cigarettes, taxes, taxes, taxes. Tax Freedom Day is a day named every year to show the impact of taxation on Canadian families if we had to pay all taxes up front for the year. Tax Freedom Day in 2010 landed on June 6th meaning, on average, we were handing over every cent we earned to the government up to that date. In 2011, the average family earned $93,831 and paid $39,960 in taxes. That tax bill represents about 42.6% of annual income. Taxes also continue to rise. In 2011 income taxes increased by $550, while sales taxes jumped by $335. No wonder people complain.

Tax expert Evelyn Jacks says, "Your tax bill is going to be your largest lifetime expense. Bigger than the amount of money that you pay on your mortgage, more than you will ever pay for cars or for your children's education. So taxation is a force to be reckoned with." Sounds a bit depressing, but if you want to accumulate, grow and build wealth in your lifetime; you need to know if there are ways to avoid paying tax. It is possible with proper planning. Jacks says, "Income taxes are really the only kind of tax that you pay that you can try to reduce. Taxes paid on alcohol, gas and cigarettes can't be changed, but when it comes to arranging your affairs, trying to pay the least amount of tax possible within the framework of the law is perfectly legal and it's your right and duty." Jacks says by being educated about the tax system allows you to keep money in your pockets instead of handing it over to the government.

You are required to file a tax return if you have taxable income. If you have a summer job that's going to pay more than $10,500, then you must file a tax return, but even if you don't make that much there are still good reasons to file a tax return. Jacks says, "You can file a tax return to start building RRSP contribution room even if it's money you made from babysitting. Eighteen percent of what you earn creates RRSP contribution room and later when you're making more money, you can contribute to an RRSP which allows you to reduce the tax you pay."

When I was younger I enjoyed doing my taxes. In fact, I used to do my Mother's as well as other family members. Now using a tax software program makes it easy. They sell for between $10 and $40 and there are even free ones online. (Just make sure they are approved for use by the government, although most of them are.) Jacks says, "Using a software program to figure out your taxes is a really good thing to do. It helps you understand the process, tax terms and it allows you to tap into your computer skills." It also takes the mystery out of the math so if you are worried about your math skills, the computer program will do it for you. What's most important is to understand how much do you earn and exactly how much do you pay in taxes. She says, "It's on line 435 of the tax return that everyone really needs to know. What did I pay in taxes this year?" Filing a tax return is not just about paying your taxes; it's also a chance to take advantage of certain benefits, such as the GST credit which people qualify for when they turn 18. "Everyone should file a tax return in their 17th year to position themselves to receive that GST credit when you turn 18." says Jacks.

If you make a mistake on your taxes in a previous year, don't worry—there is a remedy for that. You can go back up to ten years and correct mistakes to tap into refunds you may have missed. You may have heard people say they've been able to cheat the taxman. Don't do it. Anyone who ever cheats on their taxes gets caught, and there can be harsh penalties up to and including jail time. Even if you owe money you should still file your tax return on time because you can make arrangements to pay what you owe over time. Jacks says, "Once people get to know more about using their tax return as a significant financial tool then they can start tax planning, which is an essential part of your total financial picture." Jacks says you want to do the following four things:

1. Earn more of every dollar you make
2. Keep your money longer
3. Transition the most money to family members later in life
4. Move your money into places where you pay the least amount of tax

It also begins with making sure you're not overpaying your taxes when you start working. The average refund in Canada is about $1,400, which means many of us are overpaying our taxes on our paycheques. Jacks says, "You want to make sure that your employer is deducting the correct amount of tax but not one cent more. Don't use your tax return as a savings device because you like to get a refund at tax time. Instead try to pay the correct amount of tax through the year and invest the rest." It's your responsibility to file your tax return on time every year and, if you can manage it, don't spend your tax refund cheque—invest it! "The one thing that young people have going for them that older people don't, is compounding time. If you start in your youth and save regularly, it gives you the opportunity to build much greater wealth in your lifetime. You'll be much further ahead if you start early then if you start later on." says Jacks.

[36]
FINANCIAL ADVISERS—
DO YOU NEED ONE?

As we crossed Canada on our Financial Literacy Task Force Tour in 2010, one thing became clear to me; people with financial advisors generally seemed to be doing better with their investments than people who didn't use one. Now, there are individuals who do have the time and expertise to spend managing their money and many are very capable. However, there are reasons why you may want to seek professional advice:

- You may not feel equipped with the financial and tax knowledge to handle your own portfolio
- You may not feel you have the time to make sure you are making the right decisions when it comes to your investments
- You may be concerned that your sources of financial information such as friends, family, colleagues, newspaper, internet or TV may not be the best way to get financial advice
- You may feel you are better off using the services of someone who has a business background and makes their living as a professional financial advisor

Another very important thing is to know how a financial advisor is being paid. Financial Advisors make money either:

- by the hour
- by flat fee
- by commissions on investment products sold
- through a percentage of assets managed on your behalf

David Stewart is with Stewart and Kett Financial Advisors in Toronto, a fee based financial advisors service. Stewart says, "We just charge for our time so people can use us for their own needs. They like the objectivity and they know we don't have some other agenda of wanting to acquire their assets under management or try to sell them a financial product. Really, the only advice we are interested in giving, is something that is going to help them." When it comes to young people and their finances Stewart says, "My worry is that young people don't really know what it is they need to know. They really have to try and become knowledgeable about all the financial tools that are available to them to help them plan for their future."

Stewart says the bulk of his clients are older and concerned about retirement planning. He says, "Part of our job is tax planning, general financial planning, how much does someone need to save, as well as how to minimize taxes and make sure wills and insurance amounts are appropriate. Basically our job is to help advise people so that over their lifetime, they don't run out of money." Stewart and Kett do have some younger clients, but that's mostly because their families have used them in the past. He says, "It's a multi-generational business in many ways. Often young people come to us because we have managed accounts for their parents or grand-parents or we have done their tax returns over the years. As they start to branch out on their own and earn income, they will come to us for financial guidance." Stewart says he is often surprised how little some of his younger clients know about RRSPs and TFSAs even if they have a good income. He says, "In my view too many young people have a very limited knowledge as to what goes into basic financial planning."

Canada's tax expert Evelyn Jacks says parents should be doing more to educate their children about financial matters and she says a financial advisor can take many forms over a person's lifetime. "I think your first financial advisor is the person who takes your first dollar and puts it into a savings account. It may be your Mom or your Dad. It could also be the person who does your first tax return. Young people should have a financial advisor, but over a lifetime they could be from a variety of sources and that's a good thing." says Jacks.

As you get older and begin saving money in RRSPs and TFSAs, and other sources using the principals of dollar cost averaging and the power of compound interest, the money you invest each month will grow. Once it reaches an amount possibly in the area of $20,000 to $40,000, then you may wish to seek the advice of a financial advisor. Andrew Cook is a portfolio manager with Andrew Cook and Associates and is a successful money manager who co-managed one of Canada's most successful resource funds. He currently manages a resource mutual fund worth tens of millions of dollars. Cook says to get the appropriate attention you will want to bring some money to the table. He says, "Some organizations will expect you to bring $30,000 to $50,000 or more to open an account. Realistically you need a threshold amount of money to get appropriate attention." Cook adds that while the investment landscape can be confusing, it's not rocket science so you may not need a financial advisor. He says, "Your decision on whether you should hire someone to look after your portfolio should be based on the amount of time you have available to monitor your accounts, your level of interest in following markets and, from a practical aspect, whether you have enough money to get proper attention from an investment advisor."

Once you have decided to hire a financial advisor, then you should interview two, three or more to find someone you are comfortable with. Check their references and credentials as you want to feel comfortable with them and trust them. "When interviewing an advisor, ask about their education, experience, investment philosophy, specialties, references, size of their client list, amount of an average client portfolio and their disciplinary history." says Cook. A good financial advisor will be in the loop on current market trends and be aware of good investment opportunities before they become widespread public knowledge. They can also talk you out of risky investments or stop you from making emotional decisions that could be hazardous to your wealth!

There is some debate over what percentage of your money should be in stocks (which tend to be riskier, but allow a greater opportunity for growth) and bonds (a safe investment with a fixed return). Some argue it should go by your age, so if you are 30 years old you should have only 30% of you investments in bonds and 70% of your investments in stocks. When you are 40 years old, you would move your money into safer territory by putting 40% in bonds and 60% in stocks, and so on as you age through to 100 years old. This is just one strategy and some conservative money managers will suggest you should never have more than 60% in stocks, while an aggressive manager might see no reason for a young person to be in bonds at all. It's why advisors have you fill out a know-your-client (KYC) form, which asks you questions about how willing you are to accept risk. With a KYC form, your advisor will be aware of your investment knowledge, market experience and financial goals. However, Cook says even when you have an advisor; the ultimate responsibility rests with you. "It is your money. You have to determine whether the advisor's advice is reasonable. If it does not make sense, don't do it." As wise Benjamin Franklin said, we must "oversee our own affairs with our own eyes and not trust too much to others. Trusting too much to others' care is the ruin of many." You must also be completely aware of how the advisor makes money off you so you are comfortable following their instructions and suggestions. For more information on choosing a financial advisor check the following websites.

- The Investment Funds Institute of Canada: www.ific.ca
- Financial Planning Standards Council: www.fpsc.ca

[37]
LIFE INSURANCE AND WILLS —
DO YOU NEED THEM?

If you are married with children, then you need life insurance. If you are single with no dependents then you don't. It's really that simple. As you get older, life insurance is something you will want to consider, but for young people starting out, it's not something crucial for your financial plan. The question you need to ask yourself is this—do you have anyone who depends on you for financial support and, if you were to die, who would look after them? Unfortunately, I did a story recently with a family that did not have life insurance. The father, a pharmacist drowned on a family vacation, and it was only then that his wife realized that there was no insurance. She had no job, the house still had a $250,000 mortgage and there were bills to pay. It was a very sad situation.

You may have heard people say "I'm worth more dead than alive" and for many of us that's true. As you get older and start a family, life insurance will be an important part of your financial plan. If you have loved ones to take care of and you died tomorrow, would they be able to stay in their current home? Would your children be able to go to college or university? If your husband or wife had to continue to go to work, would there be enough money to pay for child and daycare expenses. Could your family live the life they had become accustomed to? If the answer is no, then you need some form of life insurance. As a single person if you did want to leave money to a niece or nephew, or make sure your funeral would not be a burden on your parents, than you may want to consider a policy with a moderate amount of $10,000 to $20,000.

Polices may be given different names by insurers, but there are generally three kinds of insurance to choose from: term, term to 100 and permanent.

- **Term:** This is the most inexpensive type of life insurance policy and for young people who do need life insurance, this is your best bet. A healthy 30 year old could get $500,000 in insurance coverage for as little as $30 a month. With term insurance you pay as you go, buying chunks of insurance in five, 10 or 20 year terms. The younger you are, the cheaper the premiums. The drawback is you don't build up equity in the plan so you could pay for 20 years and not use it (which is a good thing!), so just keep in mind if you don't die or stop paying premiums, you don't get any money back.

- **Term to 100** is a basically unending, no frills term insurance. This kind of plan can provide you protection until you are 100 years old if kept in force. The premium cost is lower than permanent polices, but again, there is no cash surrender value.

- **Permanent:** Permanent life insurance is also known as whole life or universal life insurance. With this kind of plan, money does build up in it as you pay every month but the premiums are pricey! You'll have to come up with a lot more cash every month and if you quit paying there will be penalties to pay. Permanent plans do cover you for your entire life and your premiums won't change, but the cash value of your policy may not equal what you've put into it for 10 to 12 years. A key problem with this kind of plan is that after a few years of making huge payments, some people decide to stop and then it hasn't been worth it. (Insurance agents are often paid a commission on permanent life insurance policies so be careful not to get talked into one unless you are sure this is what you want to do.)

My advice is buy term insurance, only if you need it, and put your money to work elsewhere.

The amount of life insurance you have should cover your mortgage, all bills and outstanding debts. This may be three to 10 times your current salary. You can buy insurance through a broker, financial advisor or a bank. You may also have life insurance through your work, so if you are not sure, check. I would also point out that if you have a mortgage you will most likely have mortgage insurance through your bank. The drawback is that as you pay down your mortgage, your mortgage insurance payments stay the same. Consider taking out a term policy for the amount your mortgage is instead and you'll be further ahead.

Always be honest on your life insurance forms! If you have a history of heart disease, smoke or wrestle alligators as a hobby, tell the insurer from the start. Once you disclose any health problems and have a policy in place, you're covered. If you don't disclose everything, the policy could be voided and your family could get nothing. Also, don't fall for those commercials on TV that say, "Hey, it's Fred and he just got life insurance!" The payments are low but so is the payout so these plans aren't worth it. For free information on life insurance check the Canadian Life and Health Insurance Association's Consumer Assistance Centre. It is a non-profit, non-sales line in French and English that has been in operation since 1973. For answers to any life insurance questions, call 1-800-268-8099 or check the website www.clhia.ca.

Does a Young Person Need a Will?

If you are a young person, you probably don't want to think about dying; most of us don't, so writing a will is probably the furthest thing from your mind. It's actually something older people put off doing as well. One could argue, if you are a single person with no dependents and only a few assets, then you don't need a will anyway. However, some experts believe as soon as someone turns 18, they should have a will. As a young person you may feel you don't have much to leave someone, but you could still have things like a car, furniture, big screen TV, music or movie collection, art, mementos, photo albums, computers, a pet, etc., so writing a will is worth considering. Having a will makes things easier in the event of a death. If you die without one, the law of the province where you live has its own rules as to who gets what. Your family may have to go to court to be appointed your executor and it could lead to problems and delays in administering your estate. It also increases the chance of a feud between family members when your intentions are not clear.

Having a lawyer draw up even a basic will is expensive, as much as $500. That's why for young people I think *Do it Yourself* will kits are a good choice. Kits can be purchased for about $20 online or through most bookstores. (Chapters has more than 10 for sale for about $20 to $30.) These will kits are often criticized as a "one size fits all" will and many lawyers argue they may not hold up in court if someone wishes to contest the will as invalid. But if you are just giving away your five year old car, a 42 inch plasma, an X-Box and a Spiderman comic book collection, this shouldn't be an issue. So a will kit is a good option as you are starting out. However if you get married, have a child or gain substantial assets, you should have a proper will drafted by a lawyer.

[38]
BE A SMART SHOPPER—
NOT AN EARLY ADOPTER

As the Consumer Reporter at CTV, I get to see all the neat stuff as it rolls out into the marketplace. Refrigerators with built in internet so you can check from the store if you need milk, robotic lawn mowers that will cut the grass for you and heated driveways so you'll never have to shovel the snow again. I have to admit, I feel a bit guilty showcasing these products to viewers sometimes, because I hope they don't think I'm encouraging them to buy them. I'm not, because I wouldn't buy any of them. It's our policy to cover products that are new and interesting and, in time, they may be worth having. I remember 30 years growing up in a small town and hearing about someone who bought a CD player that could play small discs that had crystal clear sound and wouldn't skip like a record. Wow, what an innovation. It was cool, but I found out the person paid about $1,000 dollars for this CD player. Within a year or so, CD players were selling for under $200 and of course now if you want one, they are about 20 bucks.

The same is true of digital cameras, flat screen TVs (boy I'm glad I waited and didn't buy one of those giant grainy heavy rear projection sets), computers and many other electronic items. I remember being with someone and watching him plunk down his credit card to pay $1,000 for an iPod. Within about a year, it was almost half the price and could hold twice as many songs. Same with the iPad. Consumers rushed out to buy the Apple computer tablet but within a year the iPad-2 was on the market and the first iPad was old news. I mention these examples because working as the Consumer Reporter, I've seen the same trends happen over and over again.

Consumers who buy the first products are known as "early adopters" and they are the ones who pay the most for something as soon as it hits the shelves, which helps pay for research and development costs. They are also the ones who are guinea pigs for new products because they end up finding all the flaws and problems which are then corrected for the next version. The first people who bought flat screen TVs paid as much as $5,000 for a 42 inch screen. Within a matter of a few years you could get a much better 42 inch TV for about $500. What I'm saying is, if you can take a deep breath and wait for the second, third or even fourth generation of any product, you'll be much further ahead. You want to hit what is known as the "sweet spot", the place where a consumer good has become popular enough to be mass-produced, the price has fallen and the design flaws and kinks have been worked out. Sometimes the sweet spot may never happen and this is a sign the product may not be worth getting. The format may not take off, the technology may become obsolete or the company may have decided to go in a new direction. You don't want to be caught with an expensive product that you can't repair or get parts for. If you want to be a smart, savvy, young consumer, never be in a hurry to buy new technology. Let the Joneses buy it first. You can always get it later cheaper and better.

[39]
BUYING USED—
SAVING MONEY

While you are building your wealth, one of the wisest things you can do is buy used items. This won't work for everything of course and there are certain things you should never buy used, but buying certain pre-owned items that are still in good shape can save you a bundle, plus the taxes too. When I first asked for quotes from successful Canadians years ago, I got a great one from Canadian rocker Sass Jordan, who topped the music charts throughout the 1980s and 1990s and later became a judge on the hugely popular TV talent show *Canadian Idol*. Jordan said, "Use one credit card, and one only. Pay it off every month. Buy pre-owned as much as possible while you build your wealth."

Even a Canadian rock star can see the value in buying pre-owned. I bought a boat a few years ago (used of course) and thought I would give water skiing another try as I remember how much fun it was in my youth. I found a used set of water skis online at a free classified website for only $50. That weekend I went water skiing and boy, it wasn't quite how I remembered... I decided not to revive my water skiing career and put the water skis back on the classified website for the same price of $50. Someone else bought them a week later. I hope they had better luck than I did, but it was no harm done. The process was much easier than buying brand new skis for $300 and then finding out I'm not the skier I used to be.

Buying used is easier than ever with the internet and free classified websites like www.kijiji.ca and www.craigslist.org. You can search for used goods right in your own community and find great deals on items that still have plenty of life left in them. If you don't mind a scratch or some wear and tear, you can find things for

137

a fraction of their original price. Need a bicycle, exercise equipment or a TV stand? Why not look and see if you can find them used for half the price of what you would pay new, saving the tax as well. With these websites the sellers are people in your area so there is no need for shipping and handling. I've personally had great luck buying rims for my snow tires and once sold a bunk bed in an afternoon that my children had grown out of. In life we go through stages, so while it's important to have that little red wagon to pull the kids in, a swing set or a hockey net, there comes a time when you don't need them, so why not sell things online to someone else who does? It's win-win. It's also a way to unclutter your home or garage and make a few bucks at the same time. If you don't want to spend anything at all you can check out www.freecycle.org. The Free Cycle Network is made up of more than six million members worldwide. It's a non-profit group that gives and gets stuff for free in an effort to reuse, recycle and keep items out of landfill sites. It's free to sign up. For more info check their website.

10 THINGS YOU SHOULD ALWAYS BUY USED

1. DVDs, CDs and books
2. Video games
3. Children's games and toys
4. Maternity and baby clothing
5. Exercise and sports equipment
6. Musical instruments
7. Office furniture
8. Self-assembly home furniture
9. Recreational toys—boats, RVs, motorcycles
10. Expensive pedigree pets

10 THINGS YOU SHOULD NEVER BUY USED

1. Children's cribs and baby furniture
2. Car seats
3. Bicycle, hockey and ski helmets
4. Laptop computers
5. Plasma and flat panel TVs
6. Digital and Video Cameras
7. Mattresses and bedding
8. Swimsuits and undergarments
9. Vacuum cleaners
10. Shoes

[40]
GETTING THE BEST DEAL ON YOUR CELL PHONE

A family phoned me at CTV looking for help because they had just received a whopper of a cell phone bill. How bad could it be, I thought? Try over $10,000! Their teenage daughter had visited Jamaica and caught up with her cousins and when she got home, she called them on her cell phone almost every night, talking for hours on end. The teen thought her plan included free nights and weekends. It did in Toronto, but not Jamaica! Not understanding your cell phone plan is one of the biggest ways people get into trouble with high cell phone bills. Unfortunately, Canada has some of the costliest cell phone rates in the world. In a study by the New America Foundation's Open Technology Initiative in 2010, they found the average cell phone plan in Canada for voice, text and data was $67.50. The U.S. was second at $59.99. In Finland you'll pay about $40.10 a month, in Japan it drops to $18.60 and in India it's just $12.90 a month.

I did a story on how to help people save money on their cell phones and that's when I met David Lemstra, who created the website www.cellplanexpert.ca. It is a great tool for helping people find the best cellphone plan and it's free. Lemstra says, "I started the website when I was looking for my own cell phone. It's crazy the way cell phones and cell phone plans are marketed. Providers keep it complicated on purpose and try to disguise high prices with hidden fees and costly add ons." The good news is, with increased competition, you can get a good deal on a cell phone and with the right plan, you can save hundreds of dollars a year.

According to Lemstra, "The worst thing you can do is walk into a store thinking the most important decision is the kind of phone you want. Don't say to a clerk I need a cell phone plan and let the sales representative decide what you should have. You should know how you are going to use your cell phone because that's what will dictate your monthly bill." Cellplanexpert.ca has a search engine that allows you to input how much you think you will be using the phone, how often you plan to call long distance and whether you want a texting or data plan. The website will then search through every plan available in your area and tell you the three best and cheapest options available. Using the website can save you weeks of research and once again, it's free. Lemstra cautions, "The first thing you should do when you get a new phone is to check the reception in your home. Usually you have up to 50 minutes that you can use on your phone, but after that they won't let you take it back. If your reception is bad, return the cell phone right away as you may need a different phone or network." As for cost, you should be able to get a good talk and texting cell plan for under $50 a month. If you have a smart phone with a data (internet) plan, you'll have to pay as much as $70. If you do very little calling, the cheapest way to own a cell phone is by purchasing a phone and using prepaid phone cards. If you need your phone for emergencies only, the website says there is actually a prepaid plan for just $3 a month! Now that's a cheap cell phone plan.

There are many mistakes people make that cause them to get a shock on their phone bill. Going to Florida for a holiday? Make sure you know how much it's going to cost to use your phone. If you are talking, texting or surfing outside your calling area, you will have to pay roaming fees and they can be very expensive. If you are going to the U.S., consider adding a U.S. roaming package before you leave. This can greatly reduce voice, text, and data rates while you're away and prevent a nasty surprise on your bill when you get back. Lemstra says, "If you need a cell phone just for the city and area you live in, sign up for a cheaper plan with a budget provider, however watch out as long distance charges may be more expensive. If you want to be on a network that will work anywhere in Canada then you'll have to go with a coast to coast provider, but they will charge you a higher price." Many young people are also saving money by not having a landline home phone. This can save you $30 to $40 a month.

For students, a cell phone presents another challenge. If you are moving away to go to school, you're going to be in a different area code so Lemstra suggests switching your number to where you're moving. He says, "Doing this will still let you keep your phone and plan. This may be a hassle but it's a way to avoid long distance charges." If you're moving from Toronto to London you can switch to a London number. Just be careful when you come home for four months because every time someone in Toronto calls you, it will be long distance. Lemstra says, "If someone is going to talk to a lot of people around the country, then you might want to consider a Canadian long distance plan which will cover your incoming and long distance calls. The only other thing you could do is switch back to a Toronto number for four months, but too much switching can become chaotic for people." When it comes to smartphones, Lemstra advises signing up for a plan and not buying the phone outright. "If you pay for your phone upfront then you're guaranteed to take a financial hit. But if you sign up for a plan, the costs will be spread out." If you've ever lost a phone you know cell phone companies aren't very forgiving. Lemstra says, "People get very upset when they have to pay $700 for an iPhone so, if you have an expensive phone and you think you might lose it or break it, then buying phone insurance might be a good idea." When signing up for any cell phone plan be prepared to bargain. Lemstra says, "There's a price war on right now. If you do your homework and use the website's free calculator you can negotiate a better deal. Mention competing plans to put the pressure on. The sales rep has authority to throw some extras in, but the people with the most authority to give you concessions are usually the phone-in sales representatives during business hours." So the next time you need to buy or renew your cell phone plan check out www.cellplan-expert.ca before you do.

COMMON CELL PHONE BILL SURPRISES

- **Texting, calling or checking voicemail while travelling**—calling while on vacation or in other countries can lead to huge extra costs on your bill
- **Roaming data charges on smart phones**—downloading information, photos and searching the internet can be costly if you're out of your area
- **Network access fees in other coverage areas**—you may have to pay other phone companies when you are out of your coverage area
- **Toll-free calls**—are not always free. You may have to use minutes from your cell phone plan that can quickly add up
- **"Free" ringtones**—ring tones may come with added costs, fees that make them not free at all

[41]
TV, INTERNET AND UTILITIES —
KEEPING COSTS UNDER CONTROL

Want a better deal on your cell phone, internet, cable or satellite? Sometimes all you have to do is ask. Why not try to lower your monthly bills because paying for these services is a huge annual cost for the rest of your life. Of course, that is unless you want to disconnect from the cell phone grid, worldwide web and TV landscape— but who wants to do that? The problem for many consumers is when they sign up for anything, they often go on autopilot and not really think about how much a service is costing them every month. I know young people who have cell phone, internet and TV service bills of more than $300 a month and that is just too much.

You should always be monitoring your expenses to see if you can get a better deal somewhere else or if you can have costs reduced with your current supplier. It's not just for these tech services either; it may be for your utilities or even fitness club contracts. I did a story about a man who signed up at a fitness club for one year and, like most people, he quit going after three months (that's the average length of time a person goes—most sign up in January with a New Year's resolution and quit by March). He agreed to have automatic payments of $35 come out of his account every month, but when he quit, he didn't notice the payments kept coming out for 20 years! That's right; this man set up an automatic payment plan and didn't notice $35 coming out of his bank account for two decades. The fitness club told him it wasn't their fault because he could have been using the gym. However, when we got involved, he got a full refund of almost $8,000. The man was so relieved, he bought groceries for a homeless shelter; still he should have been watching his bank account more carefully.

143

As a smart, savvy consumer you should always be watching where your money goes and be careful of automatic withdrawal plans because you could have extra cash coming out of your account without knowing it. I also don't believe in signing up with electricity or gas companies on "equal billing" plans where they attempt to average out the cost of your heating bill for the whole year, so you won't have high bills in the winter and lower ones in the summer. Often these averages are wrong and you may have to pay a bill at year end to make up the difference. Also, while your heating costs are higher in the winter, your cooling costs are higher in the summer so they kind of average themselves out anyway. I believe it's much better to pay your actual monthly cost, because if you find your bill is too high then you'll turn down the heat and put on a sweater.

When it comes to certain utilities you are limited by competition (don't sign up with energy marketers or hot water heater sales staff at your door), but when it comes to internet, TV and cell and home phone services, there are many different choices as companies are competing for your business. Use the internet to view what services are available and the pricing packages being offered. Take a close look at all your services as well to see if you really need everything you are paying for. Do you actually need 1,000 long distance minutes a month? When is the last time you watched the Science Fiction channel? Do you have to have the ultimate internet package or would high speed light do? Once you examine your bills closely you would be surprised how much you can save each month.

Call a competitor and say that you are unhappy with your current provider and want to switch to their company. What is the best offer they can give you? Write it down and call several others as well. Do it for every service you have that offers competition. Next call your existing provider and say that you feel you are paying too much for their service and have decided to switch to another company. This only works if you are not in a long term contract. If you are, you will have to wait until your contract is up, but that will also give you more leverage when you say you are going to switch.

These companies do not want to lose you as a customer. When you say you plan to leave, they will automatically put you through to their customer retention department, or if they don't, ask to speak to a manager. Tell them you have been offered a better rate by a competing company (and it helps if you have written down competing offers as proof you have been looking around). You may find that a better package at a lower price is suddenly available. Always be polite and calm as raising your voice or getting angry doesn't help. I recommend going through this process with all your providers at least once a year. You would be surprised how often you will either get a discount or a bump in services. If you can save $20 a month—that's $240 a year. Even if you don't get a better deal than you already have, you will know you are paying the best possible price for your services and there is some comfort in that too.

[42]
EATING SMART—
TRIMMING THE GROCERY BILL

Many people will spend months shopping for a flat screen TV to try and save $100, but then not give a second thought to buying groceries. You may only buy a TV every five years, but you will need to buy groceries every week! Unfortunately food prices are on the rise and "foodflation" will continue to have a major impact on household budgets. Changes in the global economy, soaring oil prices, growing consumer demand in China, India and Brazil and weather related droughts, flooding and disasters have led to a "perfect storm" of rising food prices. Companies are either jacking up prices or hiding price hikes by shrinking the size of their products. Restaurants are also either increasing menu prices or reducing the size of their portions.

I first met Canada's "Coupon Queen", Kimberley Clancy, when I did a story for *Canada AM* on saving money on your grocery bill. We went on a shopping trip and without using coupons, I spent $133.89. With coupons, buying the exact same items, Clancy spent just $23.45! I wouldn't have believed it if I didn't see it myself. Clancy's website, www.frugalshopper.ca is a place where anyone can go to find out about coupons, sales, and flyers as well as take part in discussion forums about how to save money on your grocery bill. As food prices rise, I wanted to ask Clancy what advice she would give young shoppers to try and save money. Clancy says, "I started a family right out of university so I had to make our budget work and that's how I got started saving money on groceries. It's something anyone can do and get better at all the time." Clancy says many people, especially young people, spend too much on dining out and convenience foods. She says, "I think that going to the grocery store and learning how to grocery shop wisely, menu plan and compare prices is a really good way to learn how to save money."

What advice would she give young people starting out? "I would say one of the best things you could do is invest in a comprehensive cook book, such as *The Joy of Cooking* or *The Good Housekeeping Illustrated Cookbook* as these books are like kitchen bibles. They discuss everything from preparing different cuts of meat to what you need to stock your kitchen to the basic things you need in order to really know how to prepare and learn about food." She says, "Young people should be less reliant on eating out and buying convenience foods because making your own food is not only cheaper, it's healthier too." She adds, "I say to everyone and this is especially important for young people, to know your prices. Pay attention to how much milk, bread and chicken costs. When you are aware of prices, it gives you the ability to check brands, compare grocery stores and browse flyers for deals." Consider buying the generic brand of most items as they are usually, but not always, made by the same manufacturer. National brands have to charge more to pay for those expensive TV commercials and magazine ads, but often it's the same corn, beans and mushrooms that go into the national brand can as it is in the generic can so it never hurts to give the cheaper one a try.

Clancy says choosing where to shop is also an important consideration. "Some premium grocery stores and high end chains have beautiful layouts, fancy displays and better lighting, but most premium outlets also own a budget grocery chain. The budget store can have prices that are 30% cheaper and the food comes from the same warehouse." Stores know that consumers are shopping around, looking for deals so many chains are now price matching the competition. Clancy says, "If you pick one discount grocer that ad matches, you can bring all your flyers to one place and still take advantage of sales." Clancy calls coupons "free money" that shoppers should take advantage of and she advises everyone to have a coupon box or wallet to stay organized. After all, saving $10 a week on groceries might not seem like much, but done every week, you can save $520 a year and smart shoppers can save much more than that. "At Frugalshopper.ca we have coupons and sale information, but one of the most important things we have is discussion forums where people share their finds, deals of the week and coupon information. Many minds make light work and if you match your coupons with sales you can get double the savings" says Clancy.

You can get coupons from newspapers, magazines, flyers, stores, booklets, grocery stores, on product packaging, mailing lists and company websites. There are now even offers on Facebook. Clancy suggests joining mailing lists on the Facebook pages of the companies with products you enjoy as sometimes they have coupon offers they send straight to their Facebook page. There are also Canadian websites where you can order coupons directly from the manufacturer like www.websaver.ca and www.save.ca.

As well as saving money buying food, there is another way to trim your grocery bill. Don't waste food! Unfortunately it is a huge problem for many shoppers. Clancy says, "When you throw out food it's like throwing money straight into the garbage and that's why everyone should be careful about what they buy and how much of their weekly shopping budget is wasted." Food may occasionally spoil or there may be something you don't like, but if you are constantly throwing out food, this is an area that you'll need to work on. Clancy says, "First figure out how much you're spending on groceries and then make an effort to scale it back. You'll eventually get better, smarter, and more aware and soon you can't help but save money. If you know you're going to buy an item every week and you see it on sale then stock up, but don't make the mistake of buying things you won't use or that will spoil."

If buying organic is important to you, shop carefully, as organic foods can be 20% to 50% higher in price than non-organic produce. There are also some organic foods that may be a better value than others. One area it may be worth buying organic is when it comes to baby food because children's developing bodies are especially vulnerable to the toxins found in nonorganic baby food. According to research done by *Consumer Reports*, children may be at risk of higher exposure to the toxins found in nonorganic food because baby food is often made up of condensed fruits or vegetables, potentially concentrating pesticide residues. Some grocery stores seeing this as an emerging market are making some organic baby foods in the same price range as non-organic brands.

For students, or anyone trying to save money, Clancy also recommends the Good Food Box Program done through food share which is a cooperative that delivers regular and organic produce boxes (www.foodshare.net/goodfoodbox). She says exploring ethnic food markets is another way to try and save as food is often purchased in bulk at significantly lower prices. She also says "buy a slow cooker as you can put in ingredients before class and dinner is ready to be served after school." Clancy says she saves thousands of dollars a year on food and you can too.

The Scanner Price Accuracy Voluntary Code

Did you know if a cash register rings up the wrong price on an item at the checkout, you may be entitled to get it for free or $10 off? The Scanner Price Accuracy Voluntary Code was introduced in 2002 and is designed to keep store checkouts in Canada accurate and honest. If the scanned price of a product at a checkout is higher than the price displayed in the store or than advertised by the store, the lower price will be honoured. If the correct price of the product is $10 or less, the retailer will give the product to the customer free of charge! Or if the correct price of the product is higher than $10, the retailer will give the customer a discount of $10 off the corrected price. So if the wrong price comes up on a can of beans—it's free. If you're buying a more expensive item like an electric drill then you're entitled to $10 off. It never hurts to watch as your goods are scanned and now you can quote The Scanner Price Accuracy Voluntary Code if the price is wrong to get a break. More than 5,000 Canadian stores have agreed to honour it.

PART FIVE

[43]
BUYING A CAR—
LOOKING AT THE BIG PICTURE

The most exciting purchase I made in my youth was my first car. It was a beat-up, grey 1972 Plymouth Satellite Sebring, not much to look at, but for me it might as well have been a Lamborghini sports car. What a great feeling it was to jump behind the wheel, pick-up friends and go wherever I wanted to. It was empowering, life changing and fun. My first car cost $700 and when I went to get car insurance, I remember it was about $1,200. I said to the insurance agent, "Excuse me, you must be mistaken. I only paid $700 for the car." But that was the price for a 17 year old male driver to be on the road. Insurance remains expensive for young drivers and when you add in maintenance, repairs, gasoline, parking and other costs you'll see that car ownership is expensive. However, the right car at the right price that is well maintained can be a great investment to help you get around and earn income.

I will dedicate several chapters to buying a car because it is often an area where people make foolish decisions and waste money. It's easy to fall for the marketer's pitch that "you are what you drive", but if that's the case, why not show that you are sensible and responsible with your money. There is nothing wrong with buying an expensive luxury car when you are older, established and can afford it, but most people starting out are not in that situation. Consider, as well, that when you buy an expensive luxury car, it's not just the car; there are additional expenses that come with it. You may have to purchase high octane premium fuel (as much as 20 cents a litre more than regular fuel), your car insurance will be higher, the hourly rate for the mechanic could be $30 dollars an hour more if you need repairs and even something as simple as an oil change could be double the price. Parts will be more expensive and harder to find and your hot set of wheels could be the target for thieves.

There are many avenues to find good quality dependable cars that won't leave you broke. We'll take a look at buying new, used and my favourite auto segment "nearly new", which is the best way to save money on a vehicle and have a car, truck or SUV that is in "like new" condition, with low kilometers and still in great shape. While some people are terrified of the car buying process there is so much research material available on the internet that finding a car is now easier than it has ever been. Also, if you find the right vehicle at a good price you'll have more money left over each month to pay off your debts faster. Before we look at buying a car, here are some issues viewers are constantly asking me about.

No Cooling Off Period!

Every week or two I get a call to the newsroom from someone who says, "Pat, you've got to help me. I just put $500 down on a car and then I changed my mind and now the dealership won't give me my money back!" I have reported on this issue many times over the years to warn the public, but people still get caught in this situation all the time. There is a ten day cooling off period when you buy things at your door (and in some other transactions like signing up at fitness clubs), but that is not the case when you walk into a car dealership and sign a contract to buy a car. A car dealer cannot keep the entire amount of a large down payment such as two or three thousand dollars, but by law they are entitled to keep an amount that they can justify they have lost as a result of holding the car for you, usually $500. Never sign on the condition of financing either because a dealer will always be able to get you financing, but it may be at a rate of 30%! Now, reputable dealerships will often return a down payment and let people out of a contract in the hope they will return in the future to buy a car when they can afford it, but many won't. So never sign a contract to buy a new or used car unless you are positive you want it or you could lose your down payment.

Buying in the U.S.

At the time of writing this book our Canadian loonie is worth about $1.06 in American money. Whenever our dollar is worth more than the American greenback, Canadians look down south to buy cars. With a population ten times ours, there are ten times the vehicles and while there can be deals, it takes a lot of time, research and depending on the car you want there may or may not be savings. The best case scenario is someone buying a high end luxury car and that's not necessarily where many young people are at when starting out in life. I interviewed Michael McAvoy of Toronto who bought a 2007 Audi S4 convertible in the U.S. He told me he saved about $15,000 over buying the same car in Canada. He used an auto broker who, for a flat fee of $1,500, found the car, did the paperwork and had the car shipped into Canada. Viraf Baliwalla of the Automall Network has a service to help Canadians buy new and used cars. Baliwalla says, "Sometimes the best deal is in the U.S., but not always. Finding the right car can take weeks or months and you need to deal with people you trust so you don't end up disappointed." As people start looking in the U.S. to buy cars, prices are being adjusted here to try and keep Canadians shopping on this side of the border.

Rust Proofing

Canadians are keeping their cars longer and every year you do, you can save thousands of dollars. Rustproofing can maintain a car's appearance, resale value and help you avoid costly repairs. This is most important if you live in a part of Canada where salt is used on the roads and is not essential if you don't. If you buy a new or used car you may be pitched an expensive rust proofing package that could add as much as $600 to $800 to the purchase price. It may be undercoating or electric modules which claim to use an electric charge to keep rust "charged" away. That may work to help bridges from rusting, but there is not enough independent evidence to show the devices work in cars. Avoid them. According to the Automobile Protection Association (APA) and the Canadian Automobile Association (CAA), the best method to keep a car from rusting is the oil spray method offered by rust proofing companies for about $100. So say no to expensive rust packages at a dealership and consider an annual oil spray. Even if it's done every other year it can be a worthwhile expense to protect your car and prevent repairs. I've done it over the years myself and find it to be something that pays for itself down the road.

[44]
BUYING A NEW CAR

B uying a new car can be an exciting purchase and it's easy to be influenced by flashy commercials and the lure of that new car smell. In the past I would never advise a younger person to buy a new car, however over the past few years, prices have come down significantly on many smaller cars targeted towards younger drivers. Many are of good quality, with great safety features and good gas mileage. There is also some comfort in buying a brand new car from a dealer that is warranted for three to five years or 80,000 to 100,000 kilometers. Of course nothing is free, so you are paying extra for this peace of mind. If you are just starting out I would strongly advise buying something in my favourite car segment "the nearly new car", but I will talk about that in the next chapter.

If you have a lot of debt, buying a new car is not something you should do. I asked Dennis DesRosiers, one of Canada's leading independent automotive consultants, what someone in debt should buy and he said, "If you are buried in debt, don't go into additional debt to buy a vehicle. A new car is one of the worst debts that you can possibly add to your ledger. If you have a high debt load and you are desperate for a vehicle, buy a beater. It's amazing how high the quality is of nine and 10 year old used cars in the marketplace." DesRosiers says if you do want to buy a new car, be informed when you enter a dealer's showroom. DesRosiers says, "It is shocking how many consumers walk into a dealership and have zero understanding on what kind of vehicle they want or the way they plan to pay for it. The worst three words you can tell a dealer are 'I don't know.' You really have to do your homework and be prepared."

If you have decided you must have a new car then you want to keep three elements in your corner; time, information and money. If you don't need a car right away you can shop around, compare the competition, take test rides in ones you like and wait for a sale or financing offer. If you don't have time and need something right away, that's when you could end buying something you don't really want and you won't have the negotiating power to get your best deal. With the internet, new car reviews, manufacturers' websites and independent publications, there is a wealth of information on vehicle pricing, fuel economy, reliability, options, comfort, space and performance. A well-researched buyer can walk into a showroom knowing as much about a car as the salesperson selling it. Before you go to buy a car you should know how you are going to pay for it. You should be pre-approved at your bank or at least have a good idea about the vehicle financing that will be offered. Too many people buy vehicles without giving consideration as to how they will pay for it. This can cause people to sign contracts that have them ending up paying more for a car then they bargained for. Zero per cent financing offers look great in those newspaper ads, but you may actually be better off taking a loan from your bank and paying cash for the car which could allow you to negotiate a lower purchase price.

Also be aware of upselling, where many car sales staff make their money. A car may have a list price of $19,999, but with added options and trim levels, plus taxes, administration fees, freight and other charges you could end up paying a total price of $35,000 before you walk out the door. Another reason to buy a two year old car is because you can avoid the massive tax hit that comes with buying new. When you buy a brand new car you will have to pay federal and provincial sales taxes, tire taxes, air conditioning taxes, energy taxes and environmental taxes. And once you pay all these fees and taxes, the car drops in price dramatically as soon as you drive it off the car lot! As soon as you turn out onto the road, your brand new vehicle is already worth about 20% less than you just paid for it. If you are buying new you also need to consider resale value. For example, a 2012 Toyota Camry purchased for $30,000 may still be worth up to 60% of its original manufactured suggested retail price or $18,000 in four years. However, a 2012 Chevrolet Impala purchased for $25,000 may be worth only 40% of its original MSRP or about $10,000 in the same time frame. So when buying brand new, consider what the car will be worth when you need to sell it or trade it in.

Fuel prices continue to rise so compare the car fuel efficiency ratings as well. The car manufacturer will give you information regarding fuel economy, but this is often overstated. The website www.fueleconomy.gov has up to date fuel ratings on every vehicle and uses real world driving ratings, not what cars can get on a machine in a lab. It's also easy to check for both new and used cars.

Another thing to watch out for is the model year. New cars are being rolled out earlier every year, so just because it's the spring of 2012 and you're buying a car, ask when the 2013 models will be out. You don't want to pick up your 2012 car only to see a 2013 model parked beside it. You may be surprised that for the same price or only a few hundred dollars more you may be able to get a car that is one model year newer which will be a big plus at resale time. Also, as I mention in the chapter on car insurance, always call your insurance company ahead of time to see how much your car insurance will be. Different makes and models will have different premiums and you don't want to find out after you sign on the dotted line that your premiums are almost as much as your car payments. I would also add, that some auto experts believe that buying a new car is actually the best car value there is as long as you keep it at least seven years. Keeping it longer than those seven years, as long as it's well maintained, will also save you money.

What to do if Your New Car is a Lemon!

Many consumers believe if they buy a brand new vehicle, it's guaranteed to be trouble free. However at CTV, I get calls all the time from people who have purchased brand new "lemons." There may be gears that stick, phantom noises that won't go away or sunroofs that leak. Most problems will be covered under warranty and should be, but there are times when dealers and car owners can't agree on whether a problem has been repaired or what the warranty should cover. If you find yourself in a battle with a dealer over warranty issues with a new car, you can contact The Canadian Motor Vehicle Arbitration Plan, also known as CAMVAP, which is an independent agency created in 1994 to resolve disputes between automobile manufacturers and vehicle owners. Best of all, it's free. The program covers disputes about defects in the assembly of the vehicle or how the manufacturer is administering the new vehicle warranty. CAMVAP requires both parties to agree to accept the decision of an impartial arbitrator as binding and final. It can order repairs to a vehicle, a buyback of the vehicle, reimbursement of repair costs, and out-of-pocket expenses up to $500. Your vehicle cannot be more than the current model year plus four years old or have traveled more than 160,000 kilometres. In 2009, the program handled 285 cases with 93 vehicles ordered to be bought back at 2.14 million dollars. Ten consumers received reimbursement for repairs they had made totalling almost $18,000 and 62 repair orders were made. CAMVAP won't be able to help you if your car was used as a taxi, limousine, hearse, snowplow or for police, fire or municipal services. They also want you to try and settle the problem with the dealer first, but if you can't, call CAMVAP's toll-free hotline at 1-800-207-0685 or check out www.camvap.ca.

[45]
LEASING A VEHICLE— BEWARE

I have never been a fan of leasing cars and have never done it myself. It was Consumer Advocate Ralph Nader who said in 1994, "Consumers are getting gouged far too often...it's more like auto fleecing than leasing." I tend to agree and never understood why someone would make a down payment of $3,500 to lease a vehicle and then pay $500 dollars a month for four years only to have to hand the vehicle back to the dealer with nothing to show for it. When the stock market collapsed in 2008, all of a sudden leasing was out of favour with car companies who were stuck with thousands of returned leased vehicles that were worth less than they could sell them for. Automakers decided leasing was history and that was it. But now—leasing is back.

Leasing is attractive because it's a way to get into a brand new car with payments of less than $300 a month on some vehicles. Make no mistake, leasing is just a long term car rental; you don't own it. It's a way to drive a car you otherwise wouldn't be able to afford, but before you decide to lease, do you really want to pay hundreds of dollars a month for years just so you can give the car back at the end of the lease to a dealer who will sell it for a profit? Do you really want to pay for wear and tear, scratches and dents and excess kilometres before giving the car to someone else? You may have an option to buy the car at the end of the lease, but it's often not a great deal and if you're going to buy it, why not buy it in the first place?

So why lease? The main reason is to have a lower monthly payment. People are also comfortable having a vehicle that is covered under warranty. It's also a way to drive more car than you can really afford. I know a couple that had an impressive pair of vehicles in their driveway; her a Japanese SUV, him a luxury European

157

sedan. Both were leased and when his job was downsized and their four years leases were up, they had nothing to show for it. They were paying over $1,000 a month in lease payments for four years and now had nothing to drive. When you lease a vehicle, you never build up equity in it the same way as if you were making loan payments. Here are some things to consider before leasing.

Lease Payments

Those ads showing leasing payments of $199 a month sure do look attractive. But once you sit down across from the person in charge of financing at the dealership, you'll quickly realize that a "capital reduction payment" of $2,900 may be required to arrive at that low monthly figure. After which, when you add in taxes, financing, administration charges and other fees, that $199 may be a lot closer to $300 a month.

Repairs

You may have to repair minor scratches and dents. Bump a fender in a parking lot? You may not mind the ding, but it will have to be repaired before you return the car at lease end.

Maintenance

Just because you don't own the car, you still have to do the required regular maintenance. Don't miss oil changes. One CTV viewer didn't change the oil for almost 15,000 kilometers and two months after handing the vehicle back, he was hit with a bill of $2,500 for engine damage.

Excessive Wear and Tear

You'll be charged for excessive wear and tear if you drive over the allowed amount of kilometers. A lease may allow you to drive 20,000 km annually for a total of 80,000 km over four years. Rack up 100,000 km and you'll have to pay for those 20,000 extra km. At 11 cents a km overage charge, that's an extra $2,200 you'll have to pay when you turn the car in. Ripped seats or a cigarette burn in the carpet will cost you extra and you could even be charged for worn out tires. One CTV viewer told me when he handed in his leased vehicle he was charged for a new set of tires. Imagine having to pay for new tires and then have to give the car to someone else.

Travel Limitations

Because your name is not on the ownership, some lease deals stipulate you can't leave your province or territory for an extended period unless you have permission from the leasing company. That's kind of like having to ask Dad for permission to have the car for the night. Who wants to relive that?

A Lease is an Iron Clad Contract

When you sign a lease you are expected to honour the contract even if you lose your job, get divorced, relocated or even die. That convertible sports car may have been a good idea when it was just you and your spouse, but with a baby on the way, you may need to switch to a mini-van. Some people think you can turn a vehicle back in if you no longer need it, but a dealer expects you to make every payment and keep your end of the bargain. If you do have to get out of a lease midway through your contract, you may have to sublease the vehicle to someone else. Companies like www.leasebusters.com bring together people who are looking to get into and out of car leases and may be worth considering if you really need to get out of a lease. Also, avoid leases that are longer than the manufacturer's warranty because you don't want to be faced with a major repair if the warranty runs out.

Types of Leases

There are generally two kinds of leases and you don't want to pick the wrong one. The most common kind used by major car companies is a closed lease which allows you to make a set number of payments during a specific time period. You make monthly payments for two, three or four years and walk away when the lease contract is complete. In an open ended lease you also make a set number of payments over a specific time frame, but when you bring the vehicle back, you could have to pay one last payment to cover the difference between "the actual value of the vehicle" and its "residual value." For example, if the vehicle had a residual value of $14,000 but the leasing company could only sell it for $12,000 you would have to pay an additional fee of $2,000. Ouch! So if you do lease, make sure it's the closed lease you are signing.

I have always said if you can't afford to buy it, you can't afford to lease it. However, I understand there are people who really do feel that leasing is for them. So here is who I would suggest would be a good candidate for leasing. If you are someone who doesn't mind having a perpetual monthly payment, want to drive a car that is always under warranty, like driving a new car every two to three years, take excellent care of vehicles and drive less than the annual kilometers allowed, then maybe leasing is for you. However, before you lease, consider the next chapter on purchasing a two or three year old car instead of leasing a new one. What you may find is that your monthly payments will be about the same and you'll also end up owning the car and not renting it which is a nice feeling indeed.

[46]
BUYING A
NEARLY NEW CAR

Other than the "old beaters" I had to buy when I was a young person, I now always buy "nearly new vehicles." These are cars that are two to four years old which I believe are the best value on the road, especially for young people starting out. As I mentioned in the chapter on buying new, a car can drop 20% of its value as soon as it's driven off the lot, so why not consider a car that is a couple of years old and nicely broken in? There are many excellent cars in the used vehicle market that have about 40,000 to 80,000 kilometers. Many are off lease vehicles which can be a great deal. On average, vehicles depreciate about 10% a year after their initial depreciation, but that really depends on the manufacturer. Typically domestic vehicles such as Ford, Chevrolet and Chrysler depreciate faster than automakers like Honda and Toyota.

A few years ago I remember buying a two year old domestic vehicle that originally sold for $24,000 for just $12,000. This has changed slightly over the years as domestic vehicles have improved and now you may have to wait until the three or four year mark to buy a domestic car for 50% of its original selling price. Some consumers are not comfortable buying used because they may feel you could end up buying someone else's problem, but that has changed over the years and you don't have to be as concerned when buying a "nearly new" car and here is why. New car quality has improved dramatically and now vehicles are made to last up to 300,000 kilometers so even when you buy a car with 100,000 km on it, it still may have two thirds of its life left. As Automotive Consultant Dennis DesRosiers told me, "New vehicles are of such high quality you can't help but end up with high-quality used cars. The invasion of high-quality Japanese vehicles forced everybody up the learning curve. So over the last decade it is unusual to have a low-quality vehicle manufactured. Just about every vehicle is currently well manufactured and that has resulted in an incredibly high-value used vehicle marketplace." Automakers like Hyundai, once known many years ago for having made the Pony which was a magnet for rust, have now also joined the big leagues building dependable high quality vehicles.

With the return of leasing there will be a new flood of leased vehicles returning to car lots in the future for resale. They can be a great value as usually they are well maintained by individuals who don't want to incur additional charges when they turn in their leased car, or by companies who have a fleet of leased vehicles which undergo regular maintenance. They are also often sold at a reasonable price point because the dealer has already made a profit on them through the leasing process. Because of its relatively young age, a nearly new vehicle will likely have few problems. These vehicles may also have some of the remaining factory warranty remaining which can also give you additional piece of mind. The last five vehicles I have purchased were all lease return vehicles between two and four years old.

One area where you may have to be careful is buying a "nearly new" former daily rental. In the past, car dealers did not have to disclose if a car was used as a daily rental but now they do, as well as if a car was used as a taxi or police cruiser (may differ in some provinces). I wouldn't want a car that was used by the police or the taxi industry (they are pretty hard on vehicles) but a former daily rental could be a good value. They are often sold below the typical asking price with about 25,000 km on the odometer. A person in the daily rental industry told me that rental cars are well maintained and looked after but that still doesn't change the fact that more than 300 different drivers drove that car and some may have either been reckless or just bad drivers. I would rather buy a vehicle off lease then a former rental car.

If you do buy a "nearly new" vehicle, it doesn't mean you won't have a repair down the road as you may. But even if you have to pay $400 for a new starter, don't forget the thousands you saved when you originally bought the car.

[47]
BUYING A USED CAR—
AVOIDING A LEMON

U sed cars are a lot more reliable now than they used to be and if you buy a good one, you can save yourself thousands of dollars. Still, no one wants to end up with "someone else's problem." There is some risk when buying a used car and the older the car and the higher the mileage means there's a greater chance you could face repairs down the road. However, you'll save money right off the bat with a lower purchase price, monthly payments and insurance costs because you are driving an older car. Also, a dent in the door of your new car may have you pulling your hair out, but that ding won't bother you as much in your used one. It's repairs that will be the biggest problem if you buy a used car with issues, so choosing one wisely, doing your research and taking your time can help you avoid getting a clunker.

There is a wealth of good information on buying used cars including *Consumer Reports Magazine*'s used car guides, the *Lemon-Aid* series of used car guides which can be found in most libraries or at www.lemonaidcars.com as well as www.canadianblackbook.com which is a wholesale and retail guide that used to be only for dealers, but now it's available free to the public. *Canadian Black Book* offers two wholesale values, a high and a low along with a guideline retail price. Another great way to check prices is to go to www.autotrader.ca which has a search option that allows you to enter the vehicle make, model and year you are looking for and the area where you live. This way you can see how many similar vehicles are for sale and what they are selling for. You may find there are 157 2009 Toyota Corollas selling for between $8,900 and $19,100. You can then compare cars with similar mileage and options. It's a great place to start your search.

Your research should include checking a model's track record, reliability, repair history and problems specific to that vehicle such as bad transmissions, peeling paint or poor steering. Whether the car is being sold as is, certified, or emissions-tested is going to be a major selling point. A car sold "as is" could have a multitude of problems, while a certified vehicle must meet certain legal standards to be considered roadworthy. You should take the car to a mechanic of your choice for an inspection. For about $100, they can tell you what kind of shape it's in and what repairs it may need in the future. They can also give you an opinion of its true value. If a seller won't allow you to take the car to be inspected by someone else—don't buy it. You will also want to have a clear idea of why you need the car in the first place. Will you be picking up the kids from daycare one block away or commuting one hour into the city every day?

You may be offered a warranty with a used vehicle purchase but I have found many of these warranties offer very limited coverage. Warranties from the manufacturer or a reputable dealer may offer some protection, but third-party warranties on small car lots are notorious for being almost worthless with many loopholes. Whether you are buying from a dealer or a private seller, inspect the vehicle carefully and if you are not a "car person", take a friend or family member along who is.

- Ask for maintenance records. Is there proof the oil has been changed regularly? Has the transmission been serviced? How old are the tires? Are there dents, scratches, rips or tears?
- If a new starter, battery or water pump was installed recently, is there paperwork or maintenance records to show it?
- Look for mismatched paint on body panels. Do panels and seams line up perfectly? Do the doors, truck and hood all open and close in good order?
- Take the car for a long test drive. Don't just go around the block. Take it out on a major highway and drive at cruising speed to see how the car feels. Is the steering tight, the alignment straight, and the drive smooth?
- Finally after running the car for a while, park it in an area with dry pavement. Check for oil, transmission or coolant leaks. If you see spots on the pavement, that's a sign there may be trouble ahead.

Of course a major concern with buying a used vehicle is whether or not it's been in an accident. A dealer is supposed to disclose if a vehicle has been in a major accident but may not. However, with the overwhelming increase of data accumulation on vehicles, consumers can now arm themselves with more information than ever before. The used vehicle information package, available from most transportation ministries for about $20, can tell you who owned the car and if it has been branded a write off by an insurance company. There are now private companies that track vehicle histories. CarProof (www.carproof.com) is a Canadian company that, for about $50, will verify the car's registration, see if there are liens on the vehicle, determine if it has ever been written off by an insurance company and check its odometer record. Whether you buy from a dealer or private seller, getting a vehicle history report is a good idea.

Odometer Fraud

When buying any used car, you need to also take into consideration the possibility of odometer fraud. That's when an odometer is unhooked and rolled back. With digital odometers a computerized tool can be used to simply type in a new odometer reading. So you could buy a used vehicle with an odometer that reads 120,000 kilometers when it's actually 180,000 km. It's estimated as many as 5% to 15% of all used cars have had their odometers tampered with. So ask for paperwork to prove the vehicle's true mileage such as oil change stickers, warranty cards and service receipts. An average vehicle in Canada is driven about 25,000 kilometer a year so if the mileage is considerably lower than this amount, there should be a good explanation as to why.

Curbsiders

Curbsiders are people who sell damaged or stolen cars which often have serious flaws and may have even been written off by insurance companies. Curbsiders often say they are selling a car for a friend or family member and usually offer to meet you at your home or at a coffee shop to close the deal. These cars may have been rebuilt, stolen or had the odometer rolled back. Always check to make sure the vehicle identification number (VIN) on the paperwork matches the number stamped on the identification plate on the dash of the car. As always if a deal seems too good to be true—it probably is.

The Kijiji and Craigslist Scam

I get calls from viewers about scammers on Kijiji and Craigslist every week. Even people who are generally wise can make dumb decisions when they find what looks like an amazing deal on a car, boat or motorcycle. Usually the scams are very similar. A car worth $12,000 is selling for just $6,900. When you write the buyer they say they are selling it in a hurry because they are going through a divorce, about to leave to go overseas or are helping out a family member with a critical illness. I've had fun with these scammers over the years writing them back and forth. One told me he had a great deal on a Ford Explorer and if I paid up front he would ship it to me for half of its true value. Where is it, I asked? You can't see it because it's in the North West Territories was the reply. No problem, I said, I have a sister in Yellowknife (I don't). Finally they get so frustrated they don't write back. In one car scam I investigated, a woman would show people a luxury car at a great price, ask for a cash down payment and then promise to return when the car was checked by a mechanic. It turned out she used a fake name and that she didn't even own the car; she just borrowed it for showings! Sadly though, I have heard from CTV viewers who have wired money to scammers, thinking they were getting a great deal on a car that never materializes. Many who are scammed are young people who have been too trusting and are new to the car buying process. There can be some great deals on these classified sites and legitimate sellers do use them because unlike *Auto Trader* and newspaper classifieds, they are free to post items for sale on. Just beware that online classifieds are the new haven for scammers, so take all the same precautions you would when buying a car any other way, including seeing it in person, never paying up front and doing a vehicle history check.

[48]
GETTING THE BEST DEAL ON CAR INSURANCE

Car insurance is getting so expensive that a young person may feel like throwing away the car keys and riding the bus. Rates have been rising steadily and now auto insurance premiums must be factored in as a huge cost of car ownership. If you haven't been driving very long, your premiums could easily be thousands of dollars a year and if you get just one speeding ticket or in one accident, your premiums could skyrocket even further. It is possible to pay less for insurance if you shop around and now that's easier than ever to do. Anne Marie Thomas is Manager of Sales at www.insurancehotline.com. Since 1994, the website has been helping drivers across Canada get car insurance quotes from competing insurers who want your business. You input information about yourself and your driving history and the website gives you the best three companies and quotes for your profile. Your current company doesn't know you're shopping around and it's a free service. The website is paid by the insurance companies if you decide to switch to their company. I have featured this website on *CTV News* and I believe it's a service that can be a real benefit to drivers.

An insurer will want to know the year, make and model of the vehicle your getting and before you buy anything, call to see how much insurance premiums will be. Thomas says, "The reason to check with an insurer before buying a car is because you may think an older car will be cheaper to insure, but a newer car may have more safety features and a lower premium. Premiums also vary from company to company. In my son's case he found his monthly payment was anywhere from between $320 to $540." Thomas says if you have an older car that's not worth very much you may want to drop collision and comprehensive coverage. She says, "If a young person bought an older vehicle that's their first car and it's only worth a few thousand dollars, maybe you don't want to buy collision coverage because you're going to have a deductible of $500 dollars. Your premiums could be $2,000 a year and in the event the car is written off in an accident, you're paying out that $500 and the maximum you're going to get in a settlement is $1,000. So take into account the value of the vehicle, less your deductible and then decide if it's worth it for collision and comprehensive insurance."

Consider the following points:

- **Increase your deductible.** If you can afford it, increasing your collision and comprehensive deductibles can save upwards of 10%.
- **Ask about discounts.** Confirm with your insurance company you are receiving all of the discounts that you are eligible for.
- Some insurance companies now offer a **5% discount if you use snow tires**.
- **Good student discount.** Some insurance companies offer a discount for a student with good grades.

One of the most important things you can do is keep a clean driving record and don't speed! If you get tickets, or are involved in an at fault accident, it can cost you for years. Thomas says, "It's a bit of a no brainer but you really want to keep a clean driving record. One accident could cause your rates to go up for six years, when you're already paying high insurance rates to start with and that can make driving unaffordable for a young person." You also want to make sure you maintain an insurance history as companies look at years of continuous insurance when rating your policy. Thomas says, "If you find you can't afford a car anymore and you decide to sell it, make sure you go back on your parent's insurance because companies look at years of continuous insurance. Also, don't let your licence lapse if you decide you can't afford to drive for a period of time because when it comes time to go back and get your licence, you will be treated as a brand new driver."

It's also important to pay your fines and parking tickets because if you don't, it could cause your licence to expire. "Parking tickets do not affect your insurance rate, but if you don't pay them you could be driving with a suspended license and not even know it. If you're in doubt, you can run a motor vehicle report on yourself (MVR) and it will tell you the status of what your licence is whether it's active, suspended or cancelled. This can be done online usually for about $15. Even if you are unaware your licence is suspended, that's no excuse and an insurance company could violate your policy and not pay out a claim in the event of an accident." You should also only make a claim when it's absolutely necessary. Don't be calling up your insurance company about scratches and dents. It can be maddening to pay for cracked windshields and a banged up side mirror, but to keep your rates down it's wise to look after minor repairs yourself. Whether the insurance company has to pay out $400 or $45,000—a claim is a claim and will be treated that way. Insurance is not meant for the small stuff. It's meant for major repairs or catastrophic loss so save the big repair bills for the insurance companies.

To get a better deal on insurance, take a driver's training course from an accredited school. Thomas says, "It saved my son about two thousand dollars in insurance. Even if you don't need the training for the insurance savings, they teach great skills that can give you security and peace of mind behind the wheel. I would encourage any new driver and anyone new to Canada to take a driver's training course." Before you throw you keys to your buddy, Crazy Larry, remember this—if you lend your car, you are lending your car insurance so if your friend has an at fault accident with your car, it could cost you for many years. Thomas cautions, "Don't let someone take your car for a spin unless you know them very well because if they smash up your car you will be on the hook for it. Accidents follow the vehicle so you could end up paying higher insurance premiums for a long time."

Another way to avoid a rate hike is to always pay your premiums. If you do not pay your premiums and they are cancelled for non-payment, it could result in an increase in your car insurance rates. Thomas says, "If you sold your car and have an insurance payment due, you might think oh well, now I don't have a car so I'm not going to bother paying it, but you have to cancel your policy properly. If you just stop making payments you will have a cancellation for non-payment on your record which will affect your insurance ratings in the future. Even though insurance is expensive for young people every year, it does get a little less costly. As you get older and gain more driving experience, your insurance premiums should get lower. It's also important to shop around to see if you can get a better rate and it can be worth it to switch because the money you save could offset any cancellation penalty you might have to pay," Thomas says. Young men continue to pay more than young women for insurance, but the closer you get to age 25 the gap narrows, and after 25 there is virtually no difference. While this has been an issue of discontent for male drivers, historically and statistically young men are more likely to get into an accident than young women. Here is another interesting fact: if you get married under the age of 25 years old, you're treated as a better insurance risk and the same as someone who is 25. (However, I don't recommend walking down the aisle in your teens just to get a break on car insurance.)

In the past many drivers have been loyal to one insurance company for decades, but it is possible to change insurance companies every year if you want to. Switching doesn't affect your premiums and is not held against you as if you are a greater risk. Thomas says, "A loyalty discount is no more than five or ten percent and if you shop around, you could save much more than that. Each insurance company targets different demographics and each insurance company's claims experience is different. Their rates are based on their claims and if they happened to have a very expensive claims year you might have to pay more. Young people should go on insurancehotline.com twice a year and midway through their renewal." If you get renewed and your rates have jumped dramatically, this could also be a sign the insurance company is charging you "go away" rates. That means your profile may not fit with their company and they want you to go away. While you should shop around anyway, if your premiums ever jump by 20 to 50%, this is a sure sign to find a better deal.

Families with a new driver should also be careful before buying a third car for their son or daughter to use. When my daughter Vanessa turned 16, I thought I would buy a small gas saver car for us to have and for her to practice with. Because we already had a car and an SUV, the insurance company told me if I added a third car, rates wouldn't change while she was learning to drive, however once she became a full time driver, the insurance for that little gas saver would be about $5,000 a year! Why? Thomas says, "If there are the same number of cars as there are drivers in a household, then each driver is going to be assigned a primary rate. This makes sense because the insurance company has more exposure because all three vehicles could be on the road at the exact same time." Boy, am I glad I called ahead. So, did Vanessa get that little car to learn in? Nope. She had better not smash up my SUV though.

Minimizing Your Car Insurance Costs

To keep your insurance costs as low as possible you need to:
- keep a clean driving record
- always keep your insurance active
- renew your licence on time
- choose the best insurance company for you
- make only necessary claims
- take only necessary coverage
- fight every ticket
- avoid being labeled "at fault" in an accident

PART SIX

[49]
BUYING A HOME

For most of us, buying a home will be the biggest investment we will ever make and you will never feel as good as crossing the threshold into your first new home. For young people, it can be a daunting task wondering how you will ever be able to come up with a down payment to buy a home, and then have the cash for mortgage payments, property taxes, utility bills and maintenance costs. After the financial crisis we have been through, there are those who believe the housing market may be overvalued and is due for a major correction. As we enter 2012 some experts are predicting a flat market, meaning prices will stay the same over the next year or two while others are predicting a drop of up to 25%! There is no doubt buying a home is a big decision which cannot be taken lightly. While over time it is generally the best investment you will ever make, if you have to sell a few years after moving into a home and the real estate market goes down, you could be in a position to potentially lose tens of thousands of dollars. Now that I have you good and scared, these are the reasons why you should buy a home as soon as you can, when you know you are going to be in an area for a considerable length of time.

As Canada's Finance Minister Jim Flaherty said at the beginning of this book when advising his triplet sons, "buy a principal residence and pay off the mortgage as quickly as you can and benefit from the tax free capital gain." When you buy a home for $300,000 and if you are lucky enough to have it increase in value to $380,000, that $80,000 is pure profit. Even though housing prices could drop, I say you have to live somewhere. Buying a home will require months and even years of research, but there are a few things that I can share with you as you begin to think about home ownership or upgrading to your second home if you have already purchased one.

Don't buy too much house. You have to be realistic. What good does it wanting a palatial mansion if you make $60,000 a year? Don't look at houses you can't afford. You may have heard the term "house broke" which refers to a person or couple who overextend themselves so much, they don't have any money left after paying all the bills associated with their home. Knowing how much you can afford is something a bank can help you with, but just because you qualify for a $500,000 mortgage doesn't mean you should take it. Generally speaking you should spend no more than 32% of your gross monthly income on housing which includes your mortgage, taxes and utility costs.

Are you going to be in the same area for an extended period of time? While I am someone who is not in favour of renting, renting makes perfect sense for young people who may not know if they will change jobs or move. You should never feel bad about paying rent if you are unsure how long you may be staying in a particular area. If you do buy a home and then have to move in a hurry, it could be a mistake that will cost you thousands of dollars.

Consider carefully if you want a house, townhouse or condominium.

While I personally am not a fan of condominiums (the last one I did a story on cost $200,000, was only 360 square feet and had a water heater in the closet; a friend of mine calls them filing cabinets for people), I realize for many young people, especially in an urban area, it is the only way they can get into the real estate market. The city of Toronto has the most condominiums per capita in the world, and because of traffic congestion in the city, they are an option if you have to work downtown to avoid commuting from the suburbs. When you buy a condo you have to realize that along with your mortgage payments, you will have maintenance fees which can increase with little notice as well as property tax payments. Condos are also usually the first units to fall in price in a real estate market correction and may fall faster and deeper than townhouses or detached houses.

A townhouse is often a better bet, especially a "freehold" townhouse where you don't have to pay maintenance fees. You will usually pay more for a townhouse than a condo and less than for a detached home, but your chance of resale may be better, especially in a down market. Price will be determined by location, location, location.

A detached home is the best choice, but affordability is the issue. Many young people will buy a condo or townhouse in the hopes of moving up to a detached home, and this can be a good strategy. I would caution that as the Consumer Reporter at CTV, I get many complaints about new home developments and I personally would not buy a condo, townhouse or home that has not yet been built. Projects are often delayed, there are issues with ongoing construction as you move into the neighbourhood, your driveway may take up to a year to get paved, you'll have to put up your own fence, and there can be general mayhem until the development is completed. This might be ok with you if you are bound and determined to have a new home; just realize there can be complications. Also, you won't know who your neighbours will be. If you buy in a mature area the trees will be grown, you can see who is already living in the area and the vast majority of work will already be done to the property. When buying a home in an established area, it's a good idea to park on the street at night or at least visit in the evening to see if it is quiet and calm or are there sirens blaring? Check with the local police and ask what the neighbourhood is like, if there are schools, a fire department and hospitals nearby. There are many things to consider when buying a home such as using a home inspector, deciding whether to sign exclusively with a real estate agent and other factors. This is just the beginning of the research you need to do. Below is the average price forecast for a home in Canada, courtesy of the Canadian Real Estate Association:

Sales Activity Forecast	2010	2010 Annual Percentage Change	2011 Forecast	2011 Annual Percentage Change	2012 Forecast	2012 Annual Percentage Change
Canada	446,936	-3.9	450,800	0.9	447,700	-0.7
British Columbia	74,640	-12.2	77,000	3.2	76,000	-1.3
Alberta	46,723	-13.6	53,350	7.3	57,000	6.8
Saskatchewan	10,872	-2.0	11,450	5.3	12,000	4.8
Manitoba	13,164	0.6	13,550	2.9	13,800	1.8
Ontario	195,591	-0.1	195,300	-0.1	188,600	-3.4
Quebec	80,052	1.2	77,000	-3.8	77,050	0.1
New Brunswick	6,702	-4.3	6,800	1.5	6,800	0.0
Nova Scotia	10,036	0.1	10,100	0.6	10,200	1.0
Prince Edward Island	1,487	5.9	1,480	-0.5	1,480	0.0
Newfoundland	4,236	-4.1	4,250	0.3	4,350	2.4

Average Price Forecast	2010	2010 Annual Percentage Change	2011 Forecast	2011 Annual Percentage Change	2012 Forecast	2012 Annual Percentage Change
Canada	339,046	5.8	363,500	7.2	363,600	0.0
British Columbia	505,178	8.5	564,700	11.8	554,800	-1.8
Alberta	352,301	3.1	357,500	1.5	364,000	1.8
Saskatchewan	242,258	4.0	255,500	5.5	256,800	0.5
Manitoba	222,132	10.3	234,700	5.7	247,100	5.3
Ontario	342,245	7.5	365,200	6.7	365,500	0.1
Quebec	248,697	8.0	261,300	5.1	269,800	3.3
New Brunswick	157,240	1.5	159,500	1.4	159,500	0.0
Nova Scotia	206,186	4.8	209,800	1.8	211,700	0.9
Prince Edward Island	147,196	0.8	147,500	0.2	148,300	0.5
Newfoundland	235,341	14.0	247,600	5.2	252,800	2.1

[50]
THE RENT TRAP

Renting is a trap some people never get out of and over the long term, it's a financial mistake you don't want to make. Most of us start off renting which is perfectly normal and acceptable to do. Moving out of your parent's home and getting your own place is one of the first steps towards adulthood. There's a sense of freedom, liberation and independence in having an apartment where friends can congregate. There is nothing quite like a place to call your own, but it comes at a price. The landlord will be at the door with his hand out every month demanding $600 to $1,200 depending on where you live and what you're renting.

When starting off in life, chances are you will have to move from one job to another to get established or change positions which could take you across town or across the country. Even if you don't move around, you may not want to buy a home right away anyway. You may not have the finances, want to make a commitment or be ready to cut the grass, shovel the walk and rake the leaves and that's completely fine. Renting is a perfectly acceptable thing to do when you are young, but you don't ever want to fall into the rent trap.

Choosing to become a lifelong renter is one of the worst financial decisions you can make. I have known people over the years that have made this mistake. One fellow I'll call Fred, is now in his 50s and has been a lifelong renter. If people are moving around or have other circumstances which prevent them from home ownership, there is nothing wrong with that, but Fred has had a good job and has lived and worked in the same area for almost 30 years. He enjoys buying the latest gadgets, taking several expensive vacations a year and dining out often. He has talked about buying a house every few years but never gets around to it. He then tells stories like, "That place I was looking at buying five years ago has gone up $50,000." But Fred never bought it so someone else has seen a $50,000 appreciation, not him. Some people may feel they are unable to buy a home because of their financial situation, but if you can afford to pay rent, then you can afford to buy a home. It's one of the most important steps you can take to secure your financial future. Your goal should always be to stop paying rent as soon as possible. You simply cannot get rich renting. You just can't.

Let's take a look at Fred's situation. He pays about $1,200 a month to rent an apartment.

If he rents for 10 years: 10 years x $1200 a month = $144,000

If he rents for 20 years: 20 years x $1,200 a month = $288,000

If he rents for 30 years: 30 years x $1,200 a month = $432,000

Over 50 years that's $720,000. That would have bought a pretty nice house!

Renting makes the landlord rich and keeps you poor. Even after paying rent for 20 years you could be asked to leave and you would have no say in the matter. That's why it's empowering to own your own home and know that you can't be evicted. Buying a home is also a great forced savings plan because you have to make payments to keep the bank happy and you will. The first year or two of home ownership can be difficult as you get used to mortgage payments, utility bills and taxes but it gets easier.

There is a double benefit that renters never see. As you pay your home off, it also increases in value. There have been dips in the real estate market in the early 1980s, early 1990s and in 2009, but over the long haul housing has always increased in value. Imagine buying a home for $200,000 and having it increase in value to $300,000. A $100,000 increase is something a renter will never see. Housing prices fluctuate, but over time increases have generally been about 4% every year. If you are paying rent don't feel bad about it, but take steps and make goals to become a homeowner. Talk to your bank because a home is the best possible investment you can make. Aside from getting married and the birth of my children, the best feeling I ever had in my life was buying my first home. There's a reason they call it "Home Sweet Home" you know.

[51]
MANAGING YOUR MORTGAGE

The largest investment most of us will make is buying a home, so negotiating your mortgage is one of the most important financial decisions you will have to contend with. If you manage your mortgage carefully you can save tens of thousands of dollars and pay off your home years sooner. Many banks want consumers to take 30 years or more to pay off their homes because that way they make the most interest off you possible. I have always been against these long amortizations and was pleased when the federal government first did away with support for 40 year mortgages and then 35 year mortgages. The maximum amortization period for a government insured mortgage now is 30 years. That's still too long, but at least it's capped so Canadians won't sign up for anything longer.

The good news for young people is that interest rates are at historic lows; however they will soon start rising. When I bought my first home in the early 1990s I paid 8.5% interest on my first mortgage. I thought that was a great deal as I remember when I was younger my brother had a car loan at 18% interest. The longer your mortgage is amortized, the more interest you have to pay, so you want to pay off your mortgage as soon as possible.

If you had a $300,000 mortgage with a 5% interest rate with a 35 year amortization you would have a monthly cost of $1,514.

A 30 year mortgage at 5% has a monthly payment of $1,610.

That's a difference of $96 per month and over the life of the mortgage that adds up to $56,139 in savings.

I believe 30 years is still too way too long. Most banks will try to automatically sign you up for a 25 to 30 year amortization without explaining all available options to you so they can keep you locked in as long as possible. I believe you should try to sign up for 20, 15 or even 10 years if possible. When I bought my first home, I amortized the mortgage over 10 years which was very hard to do and I had to extend it by a few years when my wife stayed home to raise our children, but I was able to save tens of thousands of dollars in interest.

Keeping track of your mortgage and interest payments is now easy to do with financial software and online mortgage interest calculators. You put in the mortgage figures to see how much you're paying in interest along with the principal you've borrowed and the amounts can be shocking. Part of the problem is that many consumers don't take enough interest in the interest they are paying. If they did, they could save a lot of money. The most obvious way to save money is to pay back your mortgage as soon as you can. By just paying a few hundred dollars more a month, you can pay off your home five to 10 years sooner.

Let's look at an example of a mortgage at $322,000 with an interest rate of 7.5% amortized over 25 years:

- $322,000 mortgage at 7.5% interest rate over 300 months = monthly payment of $2,356
- Total amount of interest paid to the bank over the term of the mortgage = $384,680

Now let's look at the same mortgage but over 20 years instead of 25:

- $322,000 mortgage at 7.5% interest rate over 240 months = monthly payment of $2,572
- Total amount of interest paid to the bank over the term of the mortgage = $295,159

The monthly payment goes up just $216, but you would save $89,521 in interest payments and have your home paid off five years sooner! Over 15 years the savings are that much greater:

- $322,000 mortgage at 7.5% interest rate over 180 months = monthly payment of $2,964
- Total amount of interest paid to the bank over the term of the mortgage = $211,530

Your payment would go up another $392, but you would save another $83,629 in interest payments and be done with your mortgage in 15 years. I know this may be hard to do, but it is good to be aware of the potential savings if you do want to try and pay off your home faster.

Accelerated Biweekly Payments

Making accelerated biweekly payments (every two weeks) is an excellent strategy because you will make 26 payments a year instead of 24. By matching biweekly mortgage payments to your paycheque, you don't end up searching for money at the beginning of each month. Using the example of a $322,000 mortgage with an interest rate of 7.5% and a 25 year amortization illustrates the savings that accelerated biweekly payments can have:

- $322,000 mortgage at 7.5% interest rate over 300 months = monthly payment of $2,356
- Total amount of interest paid to the bank over the term of the mortgage = $384,680

With accelerated biweekly payments...

- $322,000 mortgage at 7.5% interest rate = biweekly payment of $1,178
- Total amount of interest paid to the bank over the term of the mortgage = $296,169

The amount you pay every four weeks remains the same as the monthly payment of $2,356. But the extra two payments each year make a huge difference. In this case the mortgage would be paid back in 20.2 years, almost five years sooner, and you would save $88,511 in interest payments. If you do take a 25 year mortgage this is your best strategy.

Lump Sum Payments

It's not always possible to put an extra "lump sum payment" on your mortgage, but those who do will see their mortgage paid off much faster and save tens of thousands of dollars in interest.

- $322,000 mortgage at 7.5% interest rate over 300 months = monthly payment of $2,356
- Total amount of interest paid to the bank over the term of the mortgage = $384,680
- Lump sum payment of $1,000 a year, every year, on their mortgage.

Doing this would allow you to pay off your mortgage in just 22 years and 10 months and pay $343,923 in interest—a savings of $40,757.

Again, I prefer the accelerated biweekly plan because it is like forced savings and once it's set up, you have to make the payments. It's easy to say you will put an extra $1,000 a year on your mortgage, but hard to do. Depending on your bank there may be other payment options available to you. Some lenders offer a 20/20 prepayment option. This allows you to increase your payments by 20% or pay off up to 20% of your original balance each year. Never be afraid to ask your lender what you can do to pay off your mortgage faster. When you renegotiate your mortgage you should always try to keep your payments the same as before. If the interest rate drops there may be a temptation to make smaller payments so you will have the extra cash left over to spend. Resist this temptation if you want to pay down your mortgage faster. Also don't skip a payment when the offer is made by your bank. It's pitched as a way to give you more spending money around the holidays, but it's just another way banks try to get more interest payments out of you in the long run. If you have a mortgage or are planning to buy a home in the future, don't treat your mortgage as "set it and forget it." Managing your mortgage carefully is one way you'll be able to build wealth faster and no one wants to gives the banks any more money than we have too.

[52]
BREAKING YOUR MORTGAGE

When you sign a mortgage with a lender, it is a binding legal document and don't expect the bank to give you a break if you lose your job, break-up with your boyfriend or decide having a home really isn't for you. Many people lock into five year mortgages or longer for peace of mind in case interest rates go up, but if you break your mortgage before the term is over, it can cost you plenty. Unfortunately, I get many complaints from viewers who have to break their mortgages before the term is up and they are shocked by how much the penalty is. Many people mistakenly believe you can get out of your mortgage by paying a three month interest penalty, but that's not how it works. You pay a three month interest penalty or the interest rate differential, whichever is greater and the IRD can be a shocker. I did a story with a woman who was going through a divorce and she had to break her five year mortgage midway through the term. She was in tears when she had to pay a penalty of $18,000.

The interest rate differential is calculated as the difference between the existing interest rate and the rate for the term remaining, multiplied by the principal outstanding and the balance of the term. Sounds complicated, but what it means is— don't break your mortgage unless you really have to or you are doing it because you want to take advantage of lower interest rates. The three factors involved in determining the IRD are: the amount of prepayment, the length of the remaining term of the mortgage, and the current interest rate associated with the remaining term. While closed fixed-rate mortgages have an interest rate differential penalty, most variable-rate mortgages do not which is an added plus of a variable rate mortgage.

Here is an example of how a lender will calculate the penalty:

Nadia has a mortgage of $100,000. She is paying eight percent and there are three years left on her five-year term. Her outstanding balance is $97,218. She is considering breaking her mortgage and taking out a new one at six percent interest rates currently being offered. Nadia would have to pay a penalty based on three months interest or the mortgage differential, whichever is higher.

The three month interest penalty equals: Outstanding balance × Monthly interest rate of Nadia's mortgage × 3 months = $97,218 × (8% ÷ 12 months) × 3 months = $1,944. The three month penalty equals $1,944.

To figure out the interest rate differential we take the interest rate on Nadia's mortgage (8%), minus the current market mortgage rate (6%): 8% − 6% = 2% (interest rate differential).

The interest rate differential penalty equals: Outstanding balance × Monthly interest rate differential × months left on mortgage = $97,218 × (2% ÷ 12 months) × 36 months = $5,833. The interest rate differential would be $5,833.

If Nadia wanted to break the mortgage, she would have to pay a penalty of $5,833 since it is the higher of the two calculations. So would it be worth it?

If she stayed with her current mortgage with a 15 year amortization:
- $97,218 mortgage at 8% over 36 months = monthly payments of $929.07
- Interest paid over three years = $22,057
- Mortgage remaining after three years = $85,829

If Nadia took a new mortgage with a three year term at 6% with a 15 year amortization:
- $97,218 mortgage at 6% over 36 months = monthly payments of $820.38
- Interest paid over three years = $16,383
- Mortgage remaining after three years = $84,068

What does all this mean? Well if Nadia decided to pay the penalty of $5,833, she would save $5,674 in interest and her mortgage would be $1,761 less with the lower rate. So Nadia would save about $1,500 dollars by breaking her mortgage and going with the lower rate.

It's important to note that breaking a mortgage can be a good thing if interest rates drop and you want to take advantage of them. However, at the time of writing this book, interest rates are at historic lows and they are more likely to rise as they can't drop much lower. As soon as there is a spread of more than 1% interest between what you are paying and current rates and you have more than one year left on your mortgage, you may want to at least consider paying a penalty to get out of it.

[53]
HOME AND
TENANT INSURANCE

If you own a home, insurance is a must in order to protect your largest investment. If you are renting you should have tenant insurance to protect you, your guests and your belongings.

Home Insurance

Just like car insurance, claims for home insurance should be made only for the big stuff. A claim large or small can cause your rates to rise and if you make two claims or more, some insurance companies will drop you. Make sure you have "guaranteed replacement cost" insurance on your home to ensure there will be enough money to rebuild it in case of catastrophic loss. If you have actual cash value coverage and your expensive flat screen TV is stolen, you won't get a brand new one. You will be given a cheque based on what it's worth now, not what you paid for it. To try and save money on your policy, raise your deductible from $250 or $500 to $1,000. This can reduce your annual premiums by as much as 10% to 30%. Having a $1,000 deductible means you will have to come up with the first grand if you need to make a claim, but in almost 20 years of home ownership I have never had to. You can also combine home and auto insurance coverage for savings. Where you live will also affect how much you pay. If you are in a low claim zone your rates will be low; if you are in a high claim zone, your rates will be higher. It's best to review your coverage regularly and shop around to make sure you are getting the best rate possible.

Tenant Insurance

If you are a renter, you should have tenant insurance. Like home insurance, it includes liability coverage and protects your possessions. It also protects you from unforeseen accidents that may damage another person or their property. It will cover you in the event someone slips in your apartment or if you damage other units in your building with an overflowing bathtub. Your landlord will have property insurance on the actual building you live in, but that policy does not protect your personal belongings, upgrades you have made to your unit or your personal liability to others. Your landlord's property insurance does not cover your furniture, televisions, computers, clothes and jewellery. If your apartment building caught fire and all of your stuff was ruined, you would be responsible to replace it. Your landlord's insurance policy would only pay for repairs to fix the actual apartment building and unit itself. I've done stories on people who have had floods or fires and didn't have insurance and the consequences can be devastating.

Home Inventory

If you did have a fire or were the victim of a break-in, could you remember everything you own? If your home burns down and you have $150,000 worth of contents coverage, you are not simply handed a cheque for $150,000. You will have to give a detailed list of everything that was lost. The fridge, dishwasher and big screen TV come to mind quickly, but jewellery, artwork, CD collections, pots and pans, curtains and all your clothing are difficult to remember. Making an inventory is time consuming, but once it's done it's easy to update. A home video camera is a quick way to take inventory but an insurance company would rather see detailed lists, receipts and serial and model numbers. Once lists are made, they should be kept in a safe place, such as a safety deposit box or left with a friend or family member. Some insurance companies offer inventory lists to help you make an accurate record of your contents.

Additional Coverage

Special items, such as jewellery or hobby collections, should be appraised to give accurate assessments of their worth. They may require "a rider," which is additional insurance. Wedding rings, collectibles or expensive bikes may have a limited payout. For example, many policies will only pay $250 per bike unless you have purchased additional insurance.

You should never leave your home with an appliance running because this is often when fires and floods occur (like dryer fires due to dirty lint traps). When taking a vacation, it can be a good idea to shut off the main water valve that comes into your home, because most floods happen when people are away. Usually a hot-water hose on the back of the washing machine or a hose connected to the dishwasher bursts. Flood damage from outside flooding is generally not covered under a home insurance policy. What usually are covered (as long as it's in your policy) are back-ups into your home originating from sewers, septic tanks, eaves troughs or downspouts. Leaks or seepage through the foundation of your home are not. If you are planning to be away for more than four days, you may have to have someone check your home, or your insurance coverage could be voided. Check with your insurer before taking a lengthy trip.

www.kanetix.ca is an insurance comparison website that allows you to shop around and compare insurance rates between various companies. It's an easy way to see if you are paying too much and it's a free service. Insurance premiums differ from company to company and each insurer's rates are unique to them and, chances are, no two are alike. When getting insurance quotes you'll want to make sure you're comparing policies with the same deductibles, coverage and limitations.

- **Multi-line discount:** Most companies offer this discount as an incentive to get your auto insurance business too.
- **New home discount:** Some insurance companies will offer a discount if your home is less than 10-years old.
- **Alarm discount:** You could be eligible if your home is monitored by a centrally monitored approved security system.
- **Claims-free discount:** Offered if you have not had a home insurance claim in the last five years.
- **Mortgage-free discount:** Available if you have paid off your mortgage and now own your home outright.
- **Age discount:** A discount on your insurance as you pass certain age milestones. If available, the qualifying age differs from insurer to insurer.

If you make any significant changes to your home such as putting in a hot tub, a wood stove or you add square footage, tell your insurance provider. You don't want something to happen and then find out your coverage has limitations because you did not make your insurer aware of the changes. For many of us, our home is our largest asset, so it's vital to make sure we are properly insured in case of a flood or a fire. Also shop around to make sure you are not paying too much. Using shopping comparison websites like www.kanetix.ca and www.insurancehotline.com are excellent tools to search for a lower rate and both are free to use.

[54]
HOME RENOVATIONS — BEWARE

Once you get your own place, one of the major temptations will be to go on a spending spree to make it feel like your own. You may want a kitchen island, a home theatre room or a hot tub on the deck. Some of these things may be great for your lifestyle, décor and your social life but are they really the best move financially? We all want to live in a cool place that's nicely furnished, but it's important not to over spend on furnishings or renovations. Renovations are a prime area for fraud. I get the calls at CTV all the time, "He seemed like a professional and he got right to work. Then he asked for money up front to buy supplies and never came back." If you are planning to hire someone to do work in your home, be very careful as this is an area where many people get ripped off. Word of mouth is your best bet to find a good contractor because if a friend or family member has had a good experience with them, chances are you will too. Avoid anyone who drops off a flyer in your mailbox or calls you out of the blue.

Always try to get at least three quotes on any major job and never pay too much money up front. A contractor may say he needs a 30% deposit to secure the job and another 30% to begin. This means you have given him more than half the money before he's done anything! If a contractor is too eager to get money before starting a job, this may be a sign they're not worth the trouble. A payment plan where you pay the contractor as the work progresses such as in 10% or 20% increments can help avoid disputes. All plans and instructions should be put in writing because verbal promises mean nothing when a problem arises. Most bad renovators are knowledgeable as to how the law works, so when you say you will call the police, they don't care. If a renovator takes $35,000 from you and does absolutely no work, it's fraud. However, if he begins the job and then quits, it's a civil matter for the courts. The police won't get involved and even if you take them to court and win, it can be difficult to get the money from them.

As for what renovations should you do, you should always renovate with resale in mind. Some projects give you more bang for your buck when you sell your home and if you fix up your place a little at a time you can enjoy the improvements.

- **Painting:** The easiest and most inexpensive way to give a home a whole new look is to paint it from top to bottom.
- **The Kitchen:** The most popular renovation area for homeowners and one of the easiest places to go overboard and spend too much. While the ultra-wealthy can spend $100,000 on a kitchen renovation ($40,000 on cabinets alone) most kitchens can get a very good makeover for about $15,000.
- **Bathrooms:** A great place where money you spend can be recouped at resale. Bathrooms can show their age fast, so even an inexpensive update can help make your home seem more modern and help at resale time.
- **Fireplaces:** A great addition for those cold winter nights and a great upgrade when you sell your home. Don't go wood burning. Sure the crackle of a fire is nice, but a natural gas fireplace that starts with the flick of a switch is the better choice.
- **Flooring:** Good flooring makes all the difference. Old, damaged floors or stained and worn-out carpet looks terrible. Hardwood or laminate floors add value to your home, but shop around as prices vary by thousands of dollars. Carpeting or tile in neutral tones can also freshen up a home and give it a modern look.
- **Finished Basement:** The best way to add extra value to a home is to add square footage. A basement is a great place to put a family room, pool table or home theatre. Whether you do it yourself or have a contractor do the job, it's worth the investment and will pay off when you put your house up for sale.
- **Landscaping:** Your home should at least be comparable to other homes in the neighbourhood. Curb appeal says a lot, especially when a potential buyer pulls up in front of your house. Low-maintenance hedges and trees, hanging baskets and a well-manicured lawn will increase your home's appeal.

Just remember when it comes to home renovations don't try to keep up with the Joneses. Many people have spent $150,000 on renovations only to have their home increase in value by about $50,000. So make sure your renovation spending makes sense.

PART SEVEN

[55]
YOUR FUTURE — BEING CAREFUL ON FACEBOOK AND TWITTER

It's so easy now to communicate with friends, family and even complete strangers. Facebook, Twitter and My Space allow you to post your thoughts and photos in an instant, but a goofy picture or inappropriate comment could come back to haunt you if you are searching for a job or even already employed. When the Vancouver Canucks lost the Stanley Cup to the Boston Bruins in June 2011, there was a massive riot causing hundreds of thousands of dollars in damage in downtown Vancouver.

A receptionist at a car dealership was caught in a three second video clip stealing clothing from a looted store. She got fired. A professional mountain biker posed in front of a burning car while wearing a T-shirt from his sponsor. The company promptly dropped him. A construction worker who listed the riots as "awesome" on his Facebook page was fired the next day. You don't have to be part of a riot to know the power of social media, but it did change the lives of those who got caught up in the looting, recorded on a cellphone and uploaded to the internet. It's now clear that what ends up online about you can prevent you from being hired or even cause you to get fired.

You can also tick off your clients. A famous tweet by a public relations executive backfired when he was visiting Memphis, Tennessee to give a paid talk at Fed Ex headquarters. Ketchum Vice President James Andrews tweeted, "True confession but I'm in one of those towns where I scratch my head and say 'I would die if I had to live here!'" The problem was that Andrews was about to give a talk that morning to Fed Ex employees on digital media. It became an international embarrassment when the tweet was copied to Fed Ex's marketing management. A round

189

of corporate apologizing followed and it has become a prime example of why you should be careful with your tweets.

Another famous tweet that backfired was when job seeker and Twitter user "theconner" landed a well-paying job from internet company Cisco, but she was not sure whether to accept. She tweeted "Cisco just offered me a job! Now I have to weigh the utility of a fatty paycheck against the daily commute to San Jose and hating the work." However, not long after the company rescinded the offer tweeting: "Who is the hiring manager? I'm sure they would love to know you will hate the work. We here at Cisco are versed in the web."

Whether it's your tweets of the day, photos from university or a blog you wrote three years ago, more employers are now digging through your online past before giving you a job. What will they find? You dancing on a bar with a lampshade on your head? Maybe a racy story with foul language? Or what if you are caught bashing the very industry you are applying for a job in? You must be very careful what you post online. Employers may feel you are a poor representative of their company by making inappropriate comments, sharing confidential information or speaking too freely about after work activities that may be best kept private. When you type something in a blog, a Facebook entry or on Twitter it becomes part of the internet universe. So saying you fudged your resume, like to drive over the speed limit or that you hate the company you work for are all potentially career limiting moves.

If you are looking for a job, you should be proactive and do some research to see what exists in the online world about you. Are there videos of you on YouTube looking less than professional? Have you taken part in blogs, forum discussions, posted dumb photos of yourself or sent tasteless email jokes to friends? To see how bad the damage is, you should Google yourself and see what pops up. Check your Twitter posts. Check Facebook. Check MSN and Yahoo. Can you take down the content? Can you erase the videos? You may be able to delete content on your own or you may have to request to have it removed especially if the information is in poor taste, inaccurate or libellous. There are now even services that claim they can do it for you. However, be aware; there are ways to retrieve material from the internet even if it's been deleted.

There are a growing number of companies that claim they can manage your reputation online and remove harmful material from the internet. I've never done a story on them, but it is an interesting concept. They include ReputationDefender, Defendmyname and Naymz. Rather than using one of these services, it's best to be very careful with what you put online in the first place. If you are on Facebook or MySpace, use privacy settings so only your close friends have access to your account. Never post things online when you are in a hurry, tired or after having a few drinks. What you write in a few seconds can be around for decades and many mistakes have been made.

Your reputation is something that can take you decades to earn and so it would be a shame to have it ruined because of a lapse of judgement, a few keystrokes and the click of a mouse. You should only write in a blog, email or on Twitter what you would be comfortable having in a newspaper for the entire world to see. If you can hold yourself to that standard, you will keep yourself from getting into trouble and keep your reputation intact.

[56]
WRITING THE
PERFECT RESUME

Whether you are a teenager looking for a summer job or a university graduate starting your career, your resume is the most important tool you have as you begin your employment search. You are competing with thousands of other job seekers and your resume is your best chance to get noticed and your foot in the door for an interview. At *CTV News* I've seen resumes piled up by the hundreds, so when you send yours to an employer, it has to be able to stand out from the crowd and make an impact on the person doing the hiring.

I recently saw a mother in a clothing store asking a manager if she could submit a resume on behalf of her son. I think if the young man actually wanted the job, he should have shown up to drop it off himself. I've also witnessed young people scribbling out hand written applications standing at a store counter and leaving them with the cashier. Did they get a call for a job? I doubt it. If you want to be taken seriously, you have to make writing a resume a huge part of your job search process and you need to find out exactly who is responsible for doing the hiring so you can make out your resume directly to them.

You may have also heard a resume referred to as a *Curriculum Vitae* (Latin for course of life), or CV. Generally speaking, a resume is a one or two page summary of your skills, experience and education that comes with a cover letter. A Curriculum Vitae is often much longer and contains a summary of your academic background as well as teaching or research experience, publications, presentations, awards, honours and other professional achievements. For a young person starting out, you'll be submitting a resume, but you'll still want to include any personal and professional achievements as well.

First and foremost, your resume must be mistake free. Double check grammar, punctuation and make sure there are no typos or other errors and if there are mistakes, don't use white out; start over. When there are 100 resumes on the hiring manager's desk, every error will send your resume deeper into the pile. The resume should be easy to read, neatly typed on good quality paper. Your contact information should be clear so they can get a hold of you easily with your home phone number, cell phone number and email.

You will want to list your education, past job experiences and qualifications, but it is the cover letter that can show your personality and enthusiasm to a potential employer. Once you complete the body of your resume with a list of your skills, education and career highlights, this can stay the same for the vast majority of your job applications. It is the cover letter that should be made different for each position you are applying for. This is crucial! You will want to Google each employer and find out about them. How long have they been in business? Have they made the news recently for any reason? Are they expanding? Where is their headquarters located? This information will not only help you as you write a cover letter, but also if you are called for an interview. When making out your resume, use similar language directly from the job posting to show you are knowledgeable about their position you are applying for. You will want to include career highlights, experiences, skills, education, scholarships, degrees, diplomas, awards, clubs, volunteerism or other experiences that could make your resume a cut above the rest.

Microsoft Works and other computer programs now have resume templates that can make resume writing much easier. You can also Google specific job position templates such as "flight attendant resume template" to see how you might be able to put your resume together. If you are really concerned that you are not up to the task, there are also resume writing services that can do it for you. Furthermore, when you complete your resume, save it as a computer file so you can easily call it up to change it or add to it. The following is an example of a good resume that I helped a young person with and it helped her get the job she applied for. (Names changed for privacy reasons.)

October 20, 2011

Dr. James Johnson
Vancouver Dental Services
12 King Street
Vancouver, BC

Hello Dr. Johnson,

My name is Rachel Smith and I am a recent graduate of the Dental Assistant Program at Algonquin College. As you will see from my resume, I have taken part in a field placement program which I greatly enjoyed. I realized being in a dental office is where I was meant to be as a professional healthcare worker.

I have always been interested in my own oral hygiene and actually enjoyed going to the dentist! You'll see from my resume that my first major was in Business when I was first considering a career in accounting. However, I now know I have chosen the right profession as a dental assistant.

I am a motivated, trustworthy person and I know that I would be an asset to your dental office. I am a team player and as you will see from my many years' experience in the service industry, I am used to working with the public on an ongoing basis. I would make clients feel comfortable and make going to the dentist an enjoyable experience.

I appreciate your time and I hope that you will consider my application for your office. If I had the opportunity to work with your practice, I would do my best to make your dental office grow and flourish.

Yours Sincerely,

Rachel Smith

Rachel Smith
Street Address
City, Province
Postal Code
Phone Number or numbers
E-mail contact

EDUCATION

Algonquin College, Ottawa, ON   Sept 2010 – June 2011
Completed Dental Assistant Program   Received Diploma

Algonquin College, Ottawa, ON   2005 – 2006
Completed first year of Business Management

Moncton High School, Moncton, NB   2000 – 2004
Completed High School   Received Diploma

DENTAL SKILLS

- Complete and update client records and documents
- Locate and identify tooth anatomical landmarks including cusps, roots and surfaces
- Knowledgeable and competent in sanitization of the operatories and all dental instruments
- Able to develop, label, store and mount x-rays
- Prepare armamentarium for topical and local anaesthetic administration
- Knowledgeable in liners, bases, varnishes, cements and bonding materials
- Able to mix impression materials, fill trays and take impressions from clients

FIELD PLACEMENT

- 60 hours of field placement at Dental Office (June 2011)
- Greeted and seated clients and got them ready for dental procedures
- Assisted with endodontics, orthodontics, prosthodontics and periodontics
- Assisted with restorative procedures and taking impressions
- Assisted with porcelain fused to metal crown preparations
- Assisted with tooth whitening procedures

HIGHLIGHTS AND QUALIFICATIONS

- Fluently bilingual (French/English)
- CPR First Aid certified
- Positive attitude, responsible and organized
- Able to quickly grasp new ideas and concepts
- Exceptional interpersonal and communication skills
- Extensive experience with the public and Smart Serve Certified
- Ability to work with a team or independently to achieve goals
- Experience in fast paced working environments

EMPLOYMENT EXPERIENCE

Server Restaurant	Ottawa, ON	2010 – 2011
Server Wedding Banquet Hall	Ottawa, ON	2008 – 2009
Server Irish Pub	Ottawa, ON	2007 – 2008
Line Cook Family Restaurant	Moncton, NB	2006 – 2007
Hostess/Cashier Tim Horton's	Moncton, NB	2002 – 2005

REFERENCES

Dr. Amanda Dentist	Phone number	Dentist at Field Placement
Dr. Bill Jones	Phone number	Professor of Dentistry
Restaurant Manager	Phone number	Manager and current employer

So what does this resume show? It's clear, concise and has a personalized cover letter that indicates the person took the time to make the resume specifically for the dentist where she was applying for the job. The cover letter shows she is interested, enthusiastic and excited about the prospect of working for the dentist. It's personal instead of "I am looking for a dental position is a dental office." Her contact information, education and list of accomplishments are very clear in bullet point form. She also uses dental terminology or "terms of the trade" to show she has the skills necessary for the position. She describes her role during her field placement, which could also be included for someone who has done an internship. She states her highlights, qualifications and employment experience. The employment does not have anything to do with the dental field but it shows she has been employed steadily and working with the public. She includes three references: the dentist where she had her field placement, her favourite professor in college who she knows will give her a good review as well as her current employer.

A good resume won't automatically get you a job, but it will get you noticed and in the door for that all important first interview. A personalized cover letter can help make the person in charge of the hiring interested in meeting you and that's when you will have the chance to make a great first impression. Use the resume provided, as well as sample resumes you can find online, to design your own resume although it will differ, depending on the kind of job you are applying for. Most importantly, always remember that especially in today's marketplace, the resume is one of the most important tools you have when looking for a job. Take it seriously and take the time to do it right.

[57]
ASKING FOR A RAISE

I know young people may have some trouble relating to this story, but it's true and it was one of my first jobs, picking up rocks. Yes, walking up and down farmer's fields and picking up stones and putting them in a tractor bucket or a stone wagon. Why? Well farming equipment is very expensive and if a rock goes through a $500,000 wheat combine it can cause a lot of damage. I know you're saying, "Pat what is the point of this story?" Ok, I'll get to it. I worked for a local farmer and he needed a group of kids to pick rocks, but he didn't know any so he asked if I could organize a rock picking team to work for two weeks before planting began.

As you may have guessed, picking up rocks is tiring, back breaking and boring work, so I called both friends, and enemies, and managed to get about 10 people to show up. When all the work was done, all of us were paid $3 an hour (that was the going rate in the 1970s). I was stunned. As soon as the others left I approached the farmer in a huff. Why was I getting the same wage as the others, I demanded? After all, they would not even be here if it wasn't for me. I called them, organized them and I got them to the field on time. I told him, "If not for me, you wouldn't have any rock pickers." The farmer, a reasonable man, agreed and gave me a raise to $3.50, but added, "Don't tell them."

I tell this story because when many young people get into debt, one of the first things they think they should do is ask for more money. They feel if only their salary was greater their financial problems would be solved, but as we learned earlier in this book it's not about how much you make—it's about how much you save. So if you are spending beyond your means you will never get ahead. If you make

$30,000 a year, but spend $33,000, getting a raise to $33,000 won't help if you then spend $37,000. At any rate, if you feel you deserve a raise, there is a right and wrong way to go about it.

I interviewed Barbara Moses, career guru and best-selling author of *What Next? Find the Work That's Right for You*, for an earlier book and what she had to say is also excellent advice for young Canadians. Moses says that asking for a raise because you are having financial problems is not only unprofessional, it's embarrassing. Moses says, "Your needs for a raise are completely irrelevant to your employer. It's how you are contributing to your company and whether you are already being fairly paid that matters."

You should never tell your employer you need more money because you bought a luxury car that takes premium gas or that you have a new girlfriend that likes to dine out a lot. You need to justify your jump on the pay scale, make sure you are worthy of a raise before asking for one and be realistic. Moses says, "You have to know what your job is worth and what your value is to your employer. Unfortunately, a lot of employees overestimate their value to a company." Are you someone who can be trusted to work unsupervised and get the job done? Or are you the whiner with a bad attitude who comes to work late and leaves early? Strive to be an ideal employee and ask yourself if you were the boss, would you give yourself a raise?

Moses says analyze your accomplishments to identify how you have contributed to your company's bottom line. She says, "Can you say to your boss, this is what I have done this year that has generated the company a significant amount of income?" Also has your workload or job function changed? "You may be described as an assistant manager when in fact you are doing manager-level work. Maybe your duties have changed but your job title has not. This can be a strategy to show your boss that you are deserving of a raise," says Moses. An interesting strategy is to simply go to your boss and say, "I want a 10% raise and I want to know what the best way is to get it." Being aggressive can show that you have the drive to get ahead.

The more educated you are and the more skills you have, the harder you will be to replace, but if you are working in a sector where skill levels are not as high, there will be a larger employee pool to draw from, making you less valuable. If you feel you are truly deserving of a raise and you don't get it, you can keep your job options open. If you don't leave you may still be remembered at budget time when raises are being allocated for the following year. Just don't say you want a raise because you can't afford your smart phone bill. After all, I got the extra 50 cents an hour for getting those rock pickers to the field on time.

[58]
FLEX YOUR SOCIAL POWER

Where and how you spend your money matters and every time you buy something, you are voting with your wallet and flexing your social power. Sometimes as consumers, we may think the spending choices we make do not make a difference in the big scheme of things, but they really do. As more consumers become vegetarians, especially younger people, we have seen a shift in grocery stores that have had to change to meet the demand and carry more vegetarian products. Restaurants have also had to adapt to put more vegetarian dishes on the menu. As more consumers demand organic foods, stores have created sections and produce aisles dedicated to organic fruits and vegetables.

It's easy to fall under the mindset that as a single individual you don't have the power to change anything, whether it's environmentally, socially or politically, but that is not true. Every time you buy something you are voting. Voting for organic or not, made with child labour or not, environmentally friendly or not, tested on animals or not. If enough people exercised their right to "vote" when purchasing items, there would be a massive change in the way products are made, sold and marketed around the world. In the documentary, *Food Inc.* which takes a close look at the food industry, Gary Hirshberg, founder of Stonyfield Farm, had this to say, "The irony is that the average consumer does not feel very powerful. They think that they are the recipients of whatever industry has put there for them to consume. Trust me, it's the exact opposite. Those businesses spend billions of dollars to tally our votes. When we run an item past the supermarket scanner, we're voting."

It's true that every item we buy has an impact, so the next time you decide to "vote" at the cash register, here are some things to consider. You may wonder how your purchase at a mall in Burnaby, B.C. or Charlottetown, P.E.I. could have an effect on someone halfway around the world. How could buying that cute top or pair of jeans really impact the working conditions of a 10 year old boy in Uzbekistan picking cotton in a field? It can be pretty complicated to connect the dots from one to the other. According to information from *Free The Children*, there are about 1.4 billion cotton t-shirts sold in North America alone each year. That's a lot of t-shirts. So it only makes sense there would be a lot of cotton fields. What's troubling is that North American companies turn to countries with lenient child labour laws to make their goods. They do this so they can pay them less than they would have to pay a North American worker. After the cotton is picked, it's shipped to a manufacturer, most likely in China and then passed along to Bangladesh for textile manufacturing. After its long journey, the t-shirts are put on container ships for North America, where they are sold by multi-million dollar corporations that make the bulk of the profits. Child labour is not only a tool for the production of t-shirts but also jeans, shoes, rugs and even mining. Right now globally, it's estimated that 218 million children around the world are being used as child labourers.

If you are interested in flexing your social power when it comes to purchasing items that were not made with child labour or sweatshops, one way to do that is to look for labels that say union made, or for labels such as Rugmark and Fairtrade, which are charities that monitor child labour practices. This is a good way to be positive that your purchase is child labour free. The idea of fair trade as a social movement has gathered momentum over the years, as companies that participate in fair trade initiatives with developing countries offer better trading conditions and pay higher prices to producers. This not only leads to better economic spin offs but also higher social and environmental standards. Fair trade products now include things like handicrafts, coffee, cocoa, sugar, tea, bananas, honey, cotton, wine, fresh fruit, chocolate and flowers.

Animal testing was a huge problem decades ago, but now many companies are careful to make sure their products are not tested on animals. However, it can still be a problem within the cosmetics industry. Fortunately, it's easy to find cruelty free products on the market without too much difficulty. A list of products that are not tested on animals can be printed off at the People for the Ethical Treatment of Animals website at www.peta.org. For example, products such as Burt's Bees, Urban Decay, and the Body Shop products are not tested on animals.

If you want to lessen your environmental carbon footprint you can do that as well by buying products that have been recycled. There are recycled paper products, motor oils, bottles, clothing and even wallets. Instead of buying disposable plastic cutlery for example, you could buy 100% post-consumer recycled polystyrene that is certified compostable. Why buy toxic cleaners dangerous to humans when you can buy biodegradable cleaners made with environmentally friendly ingredients that are safer for human health. There are many products that are now certified ecologically safe. EcoLogo is a label program started by the government of Canada in 1988 but it is now recognized around the world as a respected environmental standard and certification mark. EcoLogo provides consumers with the assurance that the products and services bearing the logo meet stringent standards of environmental leadership (www.ecologo.org).

The Energy Star logo is another symbol that shows a product is the most energy efficient within its category which means you will help reduce greenhouse gas emissions and save money (www.energystar.gov).

The Green Seal logo is also a symbol that can help you recognize green products. Green Seal is a non-profit agency with a vision for a completely green economy. Based in the U.S., the logo has come to represent unquestionably green products and services (www.greenseal.org).

Before you buy something, you may want to ask yourself the following three questions:

1. **Reduce:** Do I really need to buy this?
2. **Reuse:** Could I borrow it from a friend first?
3. **Recycle:** Could I buy it second hand instead of new?

When thinking of your carbon footprint when buying food, think of these three things:

1. Can I buy local?
2. Can I buy organic?
3. Can I buy in season?

This book is about saving money as well, but as more people buy locally and organic, prices should continue to come down. Also, you want to feel good about the choices you make and flexing your social power and thinking about how you are voting at the cash register will make a difference.

Thanks to my environmentally and socially conscious daughter Vanessa who helped research and set the tone for this chapter.

[59]
GIVING TO CHARITY— VOLUNTEER TOURISM

When it comes to giving, Canadians are among the most generous people in the world. The World Giving Index finds we are tied in third place with Ireland when it comes to charitable donations. There are some who believe that everyone should donate one third of their income, spend a third and save a third. While this a noble goal, I believe it is not possible for young people starting out in life. The story of the *Good Samaritan* is a parable about a man who finds a traveller beaten and robbed on the side of the road. Others had passed him by, but the Good Samaritan stopped to help and gave him food and shelter. It was Margaret Thatcher, the Conservative Prime Minister of the United Kingdom who served from 1979 to 1990 who said, "No one would remember the Good Samaritan if he'd only had good intentions; he had money as well."

The truth is you can't take it with you and having all the money in the world will not make you a happy person so it's important to give back to society. I do however believe that it's important first to eliminate wasteful spending and have your own financial affairs in order before becoming extremely charitable. As Thatcher, known as "The Iron Lady", would say, you need money to go with those good intentions. We should all donate what we can, when we can, to a local school, church, food bank, shelter, library or hospital. You may also decide to sponsor a child in a third-world country. If you do, you will realize that it is truly better to give than to receive.

If you look after your money, your good habits will allow you to have extra funds set aside to help others. If you have a credit card bill of $2,000 with an annual interest rate of 19%, you are giving more than $31 a month or $380 a year in interest charges to your credit card company and believe me, they are not sending that money to any charity. Imagine if that credit card was paid off and you could use that $31 a month to sponsor a child stuck in poverty. You could help them enjoy a better life, go to school and get health care. Our family sponsored a child in Zimbabwe through World Vision Canada. His name is Sibanda Nkosiyapha and we sent his family $35 a month for almost 10 years. When Sibanda got older, we decided to start again with another child through Christian Children's Fund of Canada. The child we sponsor now is Marlon Talavera and he lives in Nicaragua. I was fortunate enough to travel to Nicaragua to meet him in November of 2010. I was excited and nervous and brought his family food and gifts. Knowing Marlon was a soccer fan, I bought him a pro style soccer ball which made him an instant hit in the neighbourhood. It was an emotional meeting and a moment I'll never forget and as the father of three girls, Marlon is now the son I never had.

I went on the trip with Philip Maher, the Director of Communications with CCFC, not only to meet my sponsored child, but to do a TV news report on Charity Gift Catalogues. It's a great concept where you purchase items out of a catalogue to help families in developing countries. Canadians are very generous; buying donkeys, chickens, goats as well as bicycles. Maher says, "We find children who are given bicycles actually do better in school. It's also safer for young girls so they don't have to spend long hours walking on the road alone." I also met a young couple named Wilber and Estelvina who had a baby girl Lucia. They were given a gift of five chickens and a pig. They said, "The chickens have made a huge difference in our lives as we now have eggs to sell and feed to our daughter. We also hope to breed the pig so we can have baby pigs to sell to raise money." Maher says, "Every gift someone in Canada purchases from our catalogue, no matter if it's a blanket, a cow or a well, gets to where it is supposed to go. We guarantee it." For more info check www.ccfcanada.ca/DonateNow/GiftCatalogue.

I was also fortunate enough to travel to Africa with World Vision in the fall of 2004. I went to Gulu, Uganda and was shocked at the conditions that people were living in. I saw entire families living in homes no larger than what Canadians might have for a garden shed. For me the trip was a huge eye-opener to the poverty that still exists in the world, as well a reminder of the wonderful life we are able to enjoy in Canada. So consider giving to charity if you can, because you will feel good knowing your hard earned money is helping people who really need it and not just filling the vaults of some large faceless corporation. When you occasionally get photos from your sponsored child you'll feel good too, and who knows, maybe one day like me you'll get the chance to meet them in person. My daughter Vanessa also has the volunteer travel bug and is saving up her money to take a two week trip to Tanzania, Africa through her high school to help with volunteer projects in the spring of 2012.

If you are interested in going on an overseas mission to help people in developing countries, Philip Maher with CCFC says you have to be realistic about what you can accomplish. He says, "Having led overseas volunteer trips, I think it is important for volunteers to realize that the advantages to overseas volunteering is to help them understand the world and broaden their horizon on the developing world." Maher cautions that even though volunteers may feel good about helping people in developing countries, he says in a week or two there is only so much impact you can have. "I view these trips as somewhat of a self-improvement course. When you arrive at a project, try to understand the country and the differences with our own society. I believe the greatest long-term benefit to volunteerism, if done in this way, will be that these same volunteers will forever be sympathetic to supporting the cause, the country and other causes like it through fund raising, charity or lobbying for human rights. Over a lifetime, I think this often outweighs any hands-on work done over a few weeks, as important as that is."

I also asked Craig Keilburger of *Save the Children* what he would suggest for young people hoping to help out volunteering around the world and he offered this advice, "Individuals looking for a new way to see the world while also making a difference may be interested in Me to We Trips. Me to We Trips offer volunteer opportunities in Kenya, Ecuador, India and China. Participants aren't just travelers visiting a new community, but are welcomed as friends and partners in creating sustainable social change." The trips allow Canadians to meet and learn from local communities, get their hands dirty building a school or clean water project, practice new language skills and work with local women's groups. Keilburger says the trips are exciting and rewarding at the same time. He adds, "Me to We Trips are a natural fit for any lifelong learner who is looking to explore the world around them and their own potential to change it." For more information: www.metowe.com/trips.

Some other websites that may be of interest include:
- www.freethechildren.com/getinvolved/volunteeroverseas
- www.volunteerguide.org
- www.projects-abroad.ca/volunteer-abroad

[60]
ENJOYING YOUR LIFE!

I hope you enjoyed reading this book and I hope it will be of some help to you as you plan your life. Money is not everything and there are people that have lots of it who are not happy, but money is important as it impacts so many areas of your life. It affects your education, your job, your marriage, your family, your vacations and your retirement. However, I believe life is all about balance. It's wise to save as much money as you can, make smart investment decisions and take advantage of all the various tax free programs available to help your wealth grow, but life is also about enjoying yourself and your family. It's not wise to go on expensive vacations three times a year, but maybe one vacation a year is justified even if it costs you money. You shouldn't eat out in restaurants three times a week, but maybe once a month or for special occasions is a good investment in your mental health. If you have a hobby or a special interest that you feel you must spend money on—do it. If you love astrology and want the best telescope you can buy, then buy it. If you love cars and feel you must have a new car and you feel it will fulfil you, then buy it. If your dream is to see the Great Wall of China, then save up money and go.

The problem is when people want it all with no regard for how much it will cost. If you want the new car, the trip to China and fine dining three nights a week then you will never get ahead. So if you do decide to splurge in one area of your life, cut back in another. Strike a balance in life, develop good spending habits and be wise with your money. Be a *Smart, Savvy, Young Consumer* and you will be on the path to financial success. Good luck and enjoy your life!

GLOSSARY OF FINANCIAL TERMS

Amortization Period: The number of years it will take to repay a mortgage loan in full. This can be longer than the loan's term. For example a mortgage can have a five year term but a 25 year amortization period.

Annuity: A contract providing for a series of payments. In retirement an annuity is usually purchased from an insurance company who then pays the purchaser a monthly amount while still alive.

Assets: Anything owned that has a monetary value. A home, cottage, building, vehicles or machinery. Assets can also include stocks, bonds and cash.

Bankruptcy: The legal process that declares a person or business to be insolvent and absolves that person's or business' debts. When a person or business can no longer pay their debts.

Bear Market: A prolonged period in which investment prices fall, accompanied by widespread pessimism. Bear markets usually occur when the economy is in a recession and unemployment is high, or when inflation is rising quickly.

Bonds: A bond is an investment in which an investor loans money to a company or government that borrows the funds for a defined period of time at a fixed interest rate. Bonds are generally considered very safe investments and are used to finance a variety of private and public projects.

Broker: Someone in the business of arranging funding or negotiating contracts for a client but who does not loan the money himself. They usually charge a fee or receive a commission for their services.

Bull Market: A prolonged period in which investment prices rise faster than their historical average. Bull markets can happen as a result of an economic recovery, an economic boom, or investor psychology.

Buying on Margin: Purchasing a security partly with borrowed money.

Canada Mortgage and Housing Corporation (CMHC): The Federal Crown Corporation which administers the National Housing Act. CMHC services include providing housing information and assistance to consumers and insuring home purchase loans for lenders.

Canada Pension Plan: CPP is a government program providing retirement, death and disability benefits for Canadians. Along with Old Age Security OAS, it makes up one portion of retirement planning.

Capital Gain: A type of profit derived by selling an asset at a higher price than that at which it was purchased. One-half of the amount is taxable as income when received.

Capital Loss: The loss that results when a capital asset is sold for less than its purchase price.

Closed Mortgage: A mortgage agreement which does not provide for prepayment prior to maturity. A lender may permit prepayment under certain circumstances but will levy a prepayment charge for doing so.

Closing Costs: Additional fees and expenses associated and due on the closing date, such as legal fees, disbursements, prepaid property taxes, condo fees or real estate fees.

Correction: A market correction is usually a sudden temporary decline in stock or bond prices after a period of market strength.

Conventional Mortgage: A mortgage loan which does not exceed 75% of the appraised value or purchase price of the property, whichever is the lesser of the two. Mortgages that exceed this limit must be insured.

Convertible Mortgage: A mortgage loan that can be changed from an open to a closed mortgage within prearranged and defined circumstances. Such as within one year to a five year closed.

Creditor: A person or business from whom you borrow or to whom you owe money.

Credit Rating: Every piece of credit history information in your credit file is assigned a rating by the credit grantor. It's your complete credit history of all your major financial transactions.

Credit Score: is a numeric value assigned by credit grantors to indicate how likely someone is to pay back a loan or credit card. An indicator of the level of risk that a borrower might represent and used as an indicator of whether someone is a good credit risk.

Dollar Cost Averaging: A principal of investing which entails the use of equal amounts for investment at regular intervals in the hope of reducing average share cost by acquiring more shares in periods of lower securities prices and fewer shares in periods of higher securities prices.

Disability Insurance: Insurance that is designed to replace earned income in the event that accident or illness prevents you from pursuing your livelihood.

Dividend: A payment made per share to a company's shareholders. Usually made in a profit making year it is done in what is deemed to be best for a company and its stockholders.

Estate Planning: The orderly arrangement of one's financial affairs to maximize the value transferred at death to the people and institutions favoured by the deceased, with minimum loss of value because of taxes and forced liquidation of assets.

ETFs: Exchange Traded Funds hold assets such as stocks, commodities or bonds, and trade at close to their net asset value over the course of the trading day. Most ETFs track an index and are often attractive investments because of their low costs, tax efficiency, and stock-like features.

Executor/Executrix: The person named in a will to manage the estate of the deceased according to the terms of the will. Without a Will the function is performed by and administrator.

Fair Market Value: The price a willing buyer would pay a willing seller if neither was under any compulsion to buy or sell. The current value of any given property.

GIC: A Guaranteed Investment Certificate is a secure investment that guarantees 100% of the original amount that you invested. Your investment earns interest, at either a fixed or a variable rate, or based on a pre-determined formula.

High-ratio mortgage: A conventional mortgage loan which exceeds 75% of the appraised value or purchase price of the property. This mortgage must be insured.

Holograph will: A last will and testament written completely in the persons own handwriting, signed at the end by the person writing the Will. Witnesses are not required for it to be considered legal.

Income Splitting: The process of diverting taxable income from an individual in a high tax bracket to one in a lower tax bracket.

Interest Rate: A rate which is charged or paid for the use of money. Often expressed as an annual percentage of the principal it is calculated by dividing the amount of interest by the amount of principal. If a lender charges a customer $150 in a year on a loan of $1000, then the interest rate would be 15%.

Intestate: Not having made and left a valid will. The term is also used to refer to a person who dies without leaving a valid will.

Liabilities: Everything you owe.

Life Insurance: Insurance you buy to make sure your family or other dependants arelooked after in the event of your death.

Living Will: If you become incapacitated this document preserves your wishes and acts as your voice in medical decisions, if you are unable to speak for yourself as a result of medical reasons.

Mortgage Loan: A loan used primarily for the purchase of real estate. The property being purchased becomes the security for the loan.

Mutual Funds: A mutual fund is an investment that pools money from many individuals and invests it according to the fund's stated objectives. You purchase units in the fund, and each unit represents a share of the total pool. Professional money managers make investment decisions on behalf of fund investors, buying and selling investments such as money market investments, bonds and stocks.

Open Mortgage: A mortgage agreement which allows the borrower to repay the debt more quickly than specified and usually without pre-payment charges.

Permanent Life Insurance: The most common types are whole and universal. Both offer lifetime protection. Renewal is not necessary as long as you pay the premiums. Whole Life has fixed premiums, fixed death benefits and a fixed cash value. Universal Life has flexible premiums, flexible death benefits and a cash value and the policyholder directs where the funds are invested.

Personal Net Worth: Total assets minus total liabilities of an individual.

Power of Attorney: A legal document that gives signing authority for your affairs to a spouse or other trusted person over property and personal care issues.

Power of Attorney for Property: A legal document that gives signing authority for your affairs to a spouse or other trusted person in case of accidental or other circumstances that leave your own unable to manage your own affairs.

Power of Attorney: Personal Care: A legal document that gives signing authority for your personal care and health issues only to a spouse or other trusted person in case of accidental or other circumstances that leave your own unable to manage your own affairs.

Principal: The amount actually borrowed.

Probate: The process used to make an orderly distribution and transfer of property from the deceased to a group of beneficiaries.

RESPs: Registered Education Savings Plan is a tax shelter, designed to help postsecondary students pay for their college and university education. The government will match a percentage of contributions made and investments are allowed to grow tax free.

Reverse Mortgage: Reverse mortgages allow individuals with equity in their homes to use it as a source of income. They can take a lump sum payment or a series of payments and use their residence as collateral. The principle and interest is repaid from the estate upon death or sale of the home.

RRIF: Registered Retirement Income Fund is a tax deferment retirement plan. You convert an RRSP into an RRIF on or before an individual reaches their 71st year. It is mandatory to withdraw all funds from an RRSP plan or convert the RRSP to an RRIF or life annuity. If funds are simply withdrawn from an RRSP, the entire amount is fully taxable as ordinary income; one defers this taxation by transferring investments in an RRSP into an RRIF.

RRSPs: Registered Retirement Savings Plan is an account for holding savings and investment assets. Introduced in 1957, the RRSP's purpose is to promote savings for retirement. Contributions to the plan are tax deductible RRSP and any income you earn in the RRSP is exempt from tax while funds remain in the plan. You have to pay tax when you cash in, make withdrawals, or receive payments from the plan.

Spousal RRSP: An RRSP where one spouse makes the contributions and claims the tax deductions, but the money goes into the RRSP for the other spouse.

Stocks: A stock is a piece of ownership in a corporation also known as a share. They are bought and sold on a daily basis with the price fluctuating depending on demand.

Term Life Insurance: You choose the number of years (the term) you are insured and the amount your survivors get if you die. Often purchased for 10 or 20 years or up to a certain age. The main features of term-to-100 policy are there are fixed premiums, fixed death benefits and there is no cash value that builds up in the plan.

TFSA: Tax Free Savings Account allows you to invest up to $5,000 a year into a TFSA. Investment income earned in a TFSA is tax-free and so are withdrawals. Unused contribution room is carried forward and accumulates in future years. You can invest in stocks, mutual funds, bonds and other investment vehicles. Contributions are not tax deductible.

Trust: A bequest or device which puts legal title and control of property in the hands of a party (trustee) for the benefit of another party (beneficiary).

Will: A legally enforceable declaration of a person's wishes relating to matters to be dealt with after his death and inoperative until his death. A will is revocable or can be amended by a codicil up to the time of death, and is applicable to the situation which exists at the time of death.

Variable-Rate Loan: Loan made at an interest rate that fluctuates with the prime.

Variable-Rate Mortgage: A mortgage loan for which the rate of interest changes as money market conditions change, usually not more than once a month. The monthly payment stays the same for a specified period however the amount applied towards the principal changes if the interest rate fluctuates.

INDEX

Advisors 17, 18, 34, 127-129
Assets 33, 41, 42, 53, 54, 77, 97, 112, 127, 128, 133, 211, 213-215

Bankruptcy 10, 29, 50, 77, 86, 87, 95-98, 211
Beck, Ted 20, 21
Bieber, Justin 14, 15
Bilyk, Luke 15, 16
Bonds 101, 111-113, 116, 120, 129, 211, 213
Bursary 72

Camp Millionaire 26, 27
Campbell, Laurie 17, 76, 84
CAMVAP 155
Canada Student Loan 69
Car insurance 46, 149, 155, 167, 169, 170, 183
Carrey, Jim 15
cell phone 46, 86, 90, 103, 139-141, 143, 194
Charity 206, 207
compound interest 14, 25, 36, 101, 105-107, 116, 128
Consolidation 61, 62
Consumers 10, 18, 38, 58, 61, 83, 87, 95, 97, 135, 136, 143, 146, 153, 155, 157, 161, 164, 177, 178, 201, 203, 212
Cook, Andrew 101, 128
Credit Canada 17, 29, 76, 84
Credit counseling 17, 23, 38, 61, 76, 77, 84, 97
Credit line 81, 82
Credit score 84-89, 91, 213

Dion, Celine 15
dollar cost averaging 109, 110, 113, 116, 117, 120, 128, 213

Emergency fund 63-65
Exchange Traded Funds (ETFs) 111, 112, 116, 213

Facebook 146, 189-191
Financial Literacy 5, 17-21, 23-26

financial worth 41-43, 45
Flaherty, Jim 5, 13, 14, 115, 171

GIC 111, 120, 213
Gordon, Ted 19

high net worth 33, 34
Identity 10, 89-91
Idol, Billy 17
Index Mutual Funds 112

Jacks, Evelyn 2, 5, 18, 123, 128

Kielburger, Craig 16

Leasing 157-159, 162
Leveraging 60
Liabilities 41, 42, 214
life insurance 131, 132, 133, 214

MacKinnon, Janice 18
Mortgage 9, 10, 14, 19, 24, 25, 34, 38, 41, 59, 60, 76, 81, 96, 103, 123, 131, 132, 171, 172, 176-182, 185, 215
Mutual Funds 35, 111-113, 214

payday loan 93, 94
Pollock, Greg 17

Renovations 81, 187, 188
Resume 39, 73, 190, 193-195, 198
RRIF 120, 215
RRSP 110, 119-121, 215
Rogers, John W. Jr. 21

Scholarship 71, 72, 194
Schwartz, Bill 18, 19
Statistics Canada 38, 67, 75
Stewart, Donald 20
Stocks 21, 35, 41, 99, 109-113, 116, 117, 120, 129, 211, 213, 214, 215
Student loans 9, 42, 59, 67-69, 76, 96, 127

Task Force 5, 17-20, 23-25, 75, 76, 127
tax return 68, 124, 125, 128
TFSA 64, 103, 110, 115-117, 121, 128, 215
The Wealthy Barber 14, 82, 103
Twitter 189-191